TRUE SPIRITUALITY & THE LAW OF ATTRACTION:

A Beautiful Symbiotic Relationship

By
Karl W. Gruber

PRAISE FOR KARL GRUBER'S BOOK

"Karl Gruber's new book True Spirituality & the Law of Attraction is one that will absolutely resonate with those who are advanced students of the Law of Attraction and spirituality, as well as those with new awareness. As an expert teacher on The Law of Attraction, 7 Essential Laws and Energy Mastery, I have witnessed Karl's growth over the decade, and he himself has become a great teacher and expert on this subject matter."

CHRISTY WHITMAN, New York Times bestselling author and Master Certified Law of Attraction Coach

"Excellent. A mind-expanding guide to a much-needed synthesis of understanding. A great book by Karl Gruber to assist awakening."

DR. JOE VITALE, featured teacher in the movie, The Secret, and world-renowned teacher of the Law of Attraction

"I'm excited to recommend Karl Gruber's new book 'True Spirituality & The Law of Attraction'! Karl brings a much needed and refreshing clarification to the Law of Attraction principles and how they truly function. Also, as a student and teacher of A Course in Miracles, I'm deeply appreciative that Karl has perfectly highlighted the true source of our creative ability - our connection with our Source. Of the many gifts offered throughout this book, you will receive a loving reminder that in truth, you are a powerful spark of the Divine with pure creative power!"

FIONA WILLIAMS - Author of 'Awakening Your Right Mind' and 'Healing from Fear and Following Spirit with A Course in Miracles'

"As a teacher of metaphysics and Universal Laws, I admire how Karl presents and has made these concepts mentally accessible for all. Whether a novice to Law of Attraction or a full-on Spiritual Gangster, this book is filled with powerful points of perspective. One can anticipate new levels of growth and awareness from this literary work. A great read and self-investment."

ELENI YIAMBILIS, Metaphysical Teacher & CEO at Kalyteros.life

"Karl's passion to uplift every reader radiates through each word in his book. Though I am not a marathon runner like Karl, I could relate to his journey to spirituality and the law of attraction as there was a sense of familiarity. This is a great book for anyone seeking more out of life, especially a deeper meaning and a divine connection to all that is. Very uplifting and inspirational. Highly recommend."

RENEE MARCOU, CEO iHeart Coaching Academy & Holistic Life Coach

---

"Being a manifestation practitioner and spiritual coach myself, I wish that I had of had this book to read when I was first starting out on my awakening experience. Karl has done an incredible job of not just explaining the law of attraction but also that of true non-dualistic spirituality in a way that those just starting out will be able to comprehend. I am so pleased and grateful to be co-creating with such an authentic and inspiring lightworker. Great job Karl."

JENNIFER MATTHEWS, Founder of Superconscious Success/Manifestation Practitioner/Spiritual Coach.

TRUE SPIRITUALITY & THE LAW OF ATTRACTION
A Beautiful Symbiotic Relationship

WORLD AWAKENINGS PUBLISHING
Columbus, Ohio USA

https://karlgruberlifecoach.com

ISBN: 978-8-9862482-0-2

COVER DESIGN:
@difrats

INTERIOR DESIGN & TYPOGRAPHY:
Luisa Torres @luisaferd

TABLE OF CONTENTS

This book is dedicated to those positive, possibility, power thinkers who paved the way before me to make this possible. And to my wonderful mentor/teacher, Christy Whitman.

"For a number of decades respected scientists in a variety of disciplines all over the world have been carrying out well-designed experiments whose results fly in the face of current biology and physics. Together these studies offer us copious information about the central organizing force governing our bodies and the rest of the cosmos.

What they have discovered is nothing less than astonishing. At our most elemental, we are not a chemical reaction, but an energetic charge. Human beings and all living things are a coalescence of energy in a field of energy connected to every other living thing in the world. This pulsating energy field is the central engine of our being and our consciousness, the alpha and the omega of our existence."

Author, Lynne McTaggart from her book, The Field

INTRODUCTION

This is a full-length version of my original 26-page eBook, *The 3 Pillars: A Simple 3 Step Process to Manifest Positive & Permanent Change in Your Life.*

During the summer of 2014 I had been contemplating why it is that many, many people could get the Law of Attraction to work some of the time, but not consistently. As a life coach who specializes in the Law of Attraction, I wanted to get to the bottom of this to help my clients to create the life they really wanted to be living. I too had struggled with this inconsistency of effect for a while. As I mulled over the "missing link" to the successful and consistent application of the Law of Attraction, I had a gradual unfolding epiphany: the key to *anyone* getting the Law of Attraction to work consistently is having a strong personal foundation for your life – one based on what I call The 3 Pillars.

You must first understand the basic concept of the Law: *like attracts like.* That is, you will draw toward you whatever you think and dwell upon consistently. Whether it seems bad or good, healthy, or unhealthy, lacking, or abundant, it *will be* sent to you. It is crucial to drop any resistance you hold toward that which you desire, so it is allowed to come to you. This is especially apparent when it is something that you strongly desire, like a soul mate, attracting financial wealth, getting a job promotion, and so on. We will delve much further into this as the book goes on.

Still trying to understand everything that was slowly dawning on me, I looked at why many people lives collapse like a building into a heap of dust. Professional athletes, actors, and politicians are good examples to look at, simply because they are so high-profile. Many of them live a seemingly awesome, abundant, happy life, and yet sometimes they crash because one or all three of their foundational "pillars" had a crack or a defect in it. When this happens, their "personal foundation" then rests on unstable ground. This keeps them from being in resonance and harmony with the Law of Attrac tion. That's not all as there are key spiritual principles and truths that play a key factor too. Their hopes and dreams of their thoughts are not in sync with the desires of their heart. However, foundational flaws affect *everyone* – not just a senator who fell from grace.

The central motivation for my writing is my study and implementation of the modern spiritual guide known as *A Course in Miracles*. This teaching has helped me to understand the total importance of walking in complete harmony with the Universal laws of unconditional love, forgiveness, and oneness in order to cement that rock-solid personal foundation of yours in place, to stand for all eternity. No matter what path you are walking right now in your life, as you read through the pages of this book you will begin to find yourself walk fearlessly with a new sense of strength, hope, and light like you may have never known before. The implementation of these key spiritual principles is the primary issue differentiating what I have to teach from most other Law of Attraction teachings.

This book will explain how essential it is to create and maintain a rock-solid personal foundation based on the 3 pillars and other eternal, non-dualistic spiritual principles. Not only will there be some eye-opening thoughts and ideas for you to chew on, but hopefully an effortless personal epiphany, too. You will learn how you can consistently live in harmony and resonance with both eternal spiritual truths and the Law of Attraction. In doing so your highest, right-minded aspirations, dreams, goals, and desires will unfold beautifully in your life.

Karl W. Gruber

Chapter 1:

Understanding Law of Attraction Basics

"...who has not yet discerned the deeper law whereof this is only a partial or approximate statement, namely that like draws to like, and that the goods which belong to you gravitate to you and need not be pursued with pains and cost?"

- Ralph Waldo Emerson

With her book and the movie, *The Secret* that Rhonda Byrne released a few years ago, the popularity of the Law of Attraction dramatically increased worldwide. Nonetheless it is still not widely understood. Let's put this principle under the microscope for a much closer look.

The basic definition of the Law of Attraction is:

"Like attracts like. That which is like unto itself is drawn."

Speaking of a microscope, that is a good way to understand what you, I and, everything, is made of – energy! That's right, *everything* is pure energy. If you were to put this book page under the view of a powerful electron microscope, and dial it down to the subatomic level, all you would see would be a mass of vibrating atoms. If you were to then take this same microscope and put your hand under it, and again focus it down to the subatomic level of viewing, again all you would see is a mass of vibrating atoms. Yes, *everything* is energy, and this includes your thoughts.

That's why it is critically important to pay attention to the power of your thoughts! Please understand that your thoughts are real energy, and one of the biggest roadblocks to utilizing the Law of Attraction, is not appreciating this fact. Many people suffer from the negative effect of their thoughts while believing they are not "real." Much of this comes from long-held paradigm "I'll believe it when I see it". Know that as you think anything a very powerful energy is released and affects everything and anyone around you. In her book, *The Intention Experiment*, author Lynne McTaggart, notes that modern science offers evidence of thought as real energy.

"At least forty top scientists in academic centers of research around the world have demonstrated that an information transfer constantly carries on between living things, and thought forms are simply another aspect of transmitted energy".

And I will go so far to say that your thoughts also affects non-living things as well since they too are pure energy. Once you come to this understanding, then you need to start being careful about what you are thinking, then focusing your thoughts on what it is you really do want in your life, and not what you don't want. The seeds of creating what you desire lie in the power of your own thoughts. With this knowledge in hand, remember that only *you* are the writer, producer, and director of your life – not your spouse, parents, teacher, or employer – only you!

Another important key to understanding how to utilize the Law of Attraction is described by Abraham in the book, *Ask & it Is Given*, your "Emotional Guidance System." The beauty of your Emotional Guidance System is its simplicity. If you feel *good*, then you are *in alignment* with that which you desire. If you feel *bad*, then you are *out of alignment* with what you really wish to manifest into your life. Truly, it is that simple. So, with your understanding of the creating power of your thoughts, and how you feel in the moment that you are sending your desires into the Universe, then this makes you a very powerful creator – the creator of the reality of that which you desire, and this is a very freeing feeling. Take the time to check in again with your thoughts and desires to find out what exactly is not lining up energetically and thought-wise. Remember, the Law of Attraction is completely objective, so this is an important aspect of attracting into your life that which you desire, that you need to pay attention to.

A great starting point is building a strong personal foundation with the 3 Pillars of your mental, physical, and spiritual aspects. As you do you will begin to see the importance of first laying down the groundwork of how the Law of Attraction operates.

Chapter Summary:

- Everything is energy
- Law of Attraction = Like attracts like
- Your thoughts are real energy
- Your Emotional Guidance System can tell you whether you are in alignment with what you desire

Chapter 2:

Duality vs. Oneness

"The nonsensical tragedy of duality is considered to be normal by all modern societies, which are themselves as mad as a hatter."

Gary Renard's Ascended Master Teacher, Arten, in the book The Disappearance of the Universe

The concept of understanding the two opposing thought systems of Duality (The World) and Oneness (Spiritual) may be one of the biggest blocks to the majority of the world's populace. As I will lay out for you, throughout these pages, you will see that it can only be through a personal merging of oneness with your true Divine Self, with All-That-Is, that the Law of Attraction will then work more and more and more consistently in helping to create and manifest the life and world which you truly desire.

The World's Dream of Duality

One need but watch the newscast on any television station, read the newspaper, or even listen to your neighbor's casual conversation to understand that the world is one of dualism. As one of the Universal Laws, the Law of Polarity, states, there are two ends of the stick – hot vs. cold, love vs. hate, light vs. dark, pain vs. pleasure, etc. This world is based on long held, deeply embedded paradigms of lack and attack, separation, judgment, guilt, sin, and deep feelings of unworthiness. From this perspective there are zero thoughts and feelings of oneness with your brothers and sisters in the world, or even with animals and plants. And this thought of duality, this separation of you from everything, persists every day of every year, century after century, millennium after millennium, and still it wanes not. It is the cause of an argument with your neighbor. It is the cause of all conflict. It is the cause of all wars. And still it wanes not.

If this life, this world is just a dream, where did this idea of separation from your Creator, and an ever-changing world where everything grows old and ceases to exist, come from? *A Course in Miracles* tells us that the Son of God had a "tiny mad idea" of separation that caused him to forget to laugh and sent him into a fantastical dream that spiraled off into an infinite range of possibilities and continual change – a dream of this separate life that is so beyond the understanding of the human mind that it is, literally, beyond any form of human rational understanding. But the main force behind this crazy dream is not remembering that your One True Self is one with its Source.

Is there a way out of this seemingly never-ending cycle of brutal duality where never shall the twain meet, nor peace shall ever abide? Yes, if you but look to the beautiful concept of Oneness with All-That-Is.

What Exactly Is Oneness?

There has been a great, and ongoing awakening by an ever-growing portion of humankind, over the last century or so. It is a spiritual awakening and a coming of the understanding that the world we live in and perceive in our everyday lives is really just a dream. This life we seem to live, based on a duality of everything, is actually an illusion we have dreamed of separation from our Source, from our Creator, from All-That-Is - from God. The belief and concept of Oneness is not even remotely new as world revered spiritual doctrines such as the Hindu Vedanta clearly state that this life is but a dream, with Oneness with our Divine Self being the one true reality.

Dr. Madan Lal Goel, a professor at the University of West Florida, explains in his paper, *Oneness in Hinduism*, that *"Hindus worship God as One Reality, One Consciousness. Behind the diversity of existence, there is Unity; behind individual souls, there is the Self. All beings are unified in that One-Self".*

More recently, in what is now being called the modern spiritual doctrine, *A Course in Miracles*, definitively and beautifully states about duality (separation) vs. oneness,

---

"What do you want? Light or darkness, knowledge or ignorance are yours, but not both. Opposites must be brought together, not kept apart. For their separation is only in your mind, and are reconciled by union, as you are. In union, everything that is not real must disappear, for truth is union. As darkness disappears in light, so ignorance fades away when knowledge dawns. Perception is the medium by which ignorance is brought to knowledge. Yet perception must be without deceit, for otherwise it becomes the messenger of ignorance rather than a helper in the search for truth."

I think that the key words in this statement are "truth is union". As we continue to look further into strengthening and shoring up your 3 Pillars, and fortifying your personal foundation, you will gain a better understanding of just exactly what "truth is union" means.

Why Is It Important to Remember My Oneness?

When I contemplate how outlandishly wacked-out, crazy, ever-changing, and decaying this illusion of this life is, where all that lives must eventually die, I simply have to say, "There has *got* to be something better than this"! Ever since

I was a small child, I inherently have known that there really *is* something better than this. This "something better" is the real reality, and that there is an existence where all really *is* One, where nothing ever changes and is totally consistent because nothing need change. When all is One you need nothing because it is already there and is always there. There is unlimited abundance of everything – love, light, perfect truth, no sickness, no guilt, no sin, no attack, no lack.

I think the best jaw-dropping description of what it is like to be back home in Oneness with our Creator and our brothers eternally sustained by All-That-Is, comes from Gary Renard's book, *The Disappearance of the Universe*, when Gary's ascended Master, Pursah, described it, "*Well, imagine the very peak of a perfect sexual orgasm, except this orgasm never stops. It keeps going on forever with no decrease in its powerful and flawless intensity*". Whereupon Gary responded, "*You have my attention*". Attention indeed!

Chapter Summary:

- Separation from our brothers and sisters, and from God is only an illusion.
- Oneness with All-That-Is is our one true reality.
- Truth is union.

"Nothing real can be threatened.
Nothing unreal exists.
Herein lies the peace of God."

- A Course in Miracles

Chapter 3:

The Ego's Tiny Mad Idea: The Genesis of Separation

If one follows the train of thought that our true self really is a Divine Self at one with All-That-Is, then the idea that we are asleep in a deep dream – a literal nightmare of murder, ever changing and decaying, where there is never enough for everyone, and plagued by unending war and pestilence, what *A Course in Miracles* calls a "tiny mad idea" - morphs into something truly beyond our puny human comprehension. This "something" is meant to drive a gap between you and your Creator, and keep you splintered off separate and feeling afraid and alone. I don't know about you, but I think this is pretty damn scary, that is if you stay stuck there not being able to see a way out or see *any* kind of light at the end of the tunnel. With all of the seeming complexity and chaos the ego throws at us on a moment-to-moment basis, believe it or not, the way out of this tiny mad idea is simple, and that is remembering that *you are not separate from your Creator!*

Lesson #113 in *A Course in Miracles Workbook for Students* (which offers 365 daily lessons of non-dualistic spiritual principles) states this definitively. *"I am One Self, united with my Creator."*

Let's take a look at this a bit closer. What does it *really* mean to be One Self united with your Creator? I think the incredible spiritual enrapturement that Dr. David Hawkins experienced as a young boy, as he writes in his book, *Power vs. Force*, goes a long way in describing it.

"In 1939, I was a paperboy in rural Wisconsin and had a 17-mile route. One dark winter's night, I was caught miles from home in a blizzard, The temperature was 20 degrees below zero, and my bicycle toppled over on an icy, snow-covered field. A fierce wind ripped out the newspapers that I carried in my handlebar basket, strewing them across the terrain...To get out of the wind, I broke through the icy crust of a high snowbank and dug out a place to burrow into. The shivering stopped and was replaced by a delicious warmth...and then a state of peace beyond all description. This was accompanied by a suffusion of light and a Presence of infinite love, which had no beginning and no end, and which was indistinguishable from my own essence. I became oblivious of the physical body and surroundings as my awareness fused with this all-present illuminated state. The mind grew silent; all thought stopped. An infinite Presence was all that was or could be, and it was beyond time or description." Hawkins, of course, survived this snowy incident, and goes on to say, *"This experience was never discussed with anyone. There was no context available with which to comprehend it; I had never heard of spiritual experiences. But after this experience, the accepted reality of the world began to seem only provisional; traditional religious teaching lost significance, and, paradoxically, I became an agnostic. Compared to the light of Divinity that I had felt bathing all existence, the god of traditional religion shone dully indeed. I had lost religion but discovered spirituality."*

This type of merging with Divinity in an all-encompassing light and an infinite Presence of unconditional love is typical of most every spiritual experience described by almost all N.D.E.'ers (Near Death Experience).

In her book, *Dying to be Me*, by Anita Moorjani, describes her near death experience and her ensuing rapture upon merging with All-That-Is, as she lay dying from cancer in a hospital bed.

"There I was, without my body or any physical traits, yet my essence continued to exist, and it was not a reduced element of my whole self. In fact, it felt far greater and more intense and expansive than my physical being – magnificent, in fact. I felt eternal, as if I'd always existed and always would without beginning or end. I was filled with the knowledge that I was simply magnificent!"

What these firsthand accounts of spiritual experiences and a merging into the infinite Oneness of God shows us just how completely insane the ego's tiny mad idea of separation really is. Upon inserting this insane dream into the thoughts of a sleeping Holy Son of God, the ego implemented its plan of divide and conquer, and thus ensued the "Big Bang"! This was the moment that the Universe as we know it was created where all is *not* one, and the deadly spiral of separation and disunity gained momentum in exchanging a dream for reality. This caused a forgetfulness in our Divine Self where the we now perceive the dream of this life as our reality, and the reality of eternal Oneness and All-That-Is-ness as the dream. *This* is the tiny mad idea.

The whole insidious plan behind the idea of a world that is ever-changing and based on lack and attack is immediately vaporized when you accept the simplicity of the resolution – *"ONE PROBLEM, ONE SOLUTION"*. This is the simple answer as stated in Lesson 80 in *A Course in Miracles*. One problem, one solution? Yes, it means the single and *only* problem that is the cause of all your problems, of all the problems in the world, is that we *think* we are separate from The Creator. The solution? Remembering that we are not, nor ever will or can be separate from The Creator.

Can it really be this simple? According to most spiritual teachings throughout history, yes. Is it easy to implement? For many, simplicity may not translate into making it easier, but it can help pave the way to your spiritual awakening by eliminating many roadblocks. In reading about the simplicity of the one, single solution of remembering our inherent Divine Self who is currently asleep in a dream of separation, it is possible to imagine. Putting this into practice within our daily comings and goings is yet another thing that may not seem so simple and easy.

"One problem, one solution. Salvation is accomplished. Freedom from conflict has been given you. Accept that fact, and you are ready to take your rightful place in God's plan for salvation".
A Course in Miracles

(Lesson 80 from the "Workbook for Students")

Fortunately, throughout the ages, there have been those few souls who have understood either intuitively or through open-minded intelligent research that this life is but a dream, an illusion.

"Our innate superstition that the world we see is the world indeed is so deeply ingrained in our nature that it will rise again and again and make us believe that our world-image is the world in reality. Our primitive illusions need to be rudely shaken before a wider knowledge can be born"

J.J. van der Leeuw

The concept that the world we see and the lives we each lead is but a dream, an illusion, is not new. It is an inherent understanding that many spiritual teachers and teachings have expounded throughout the ages. With this understanding, even when faced with scientific proof that the world is but a dream and what we consider to be solid matter, the vast majority of the world's population simply considers it to be mumbo jumbo.

As pointed out by author Brendan D. Murphy in his book, *The Grand Illusion: A Synthesis of Science and Spirituality, Book One*,

"Today it is increasingly well recognized that so-called physical matter is actually standing waves, congealed light, or as David Bohm {One of the world's greatest quantum physicists} *referred to it, frozen light."*

Murphy goes on to note a quote from Dr. Len Horowitz that humans are "crystallized or precipitated light." And Murphy then concludes with a quote from Einstein, "*We have been all wrong. What we have called matter is energy, whose vibration has been so lowered as to be perceptible to the senses. There is no matter.*"

The point is that for much of modern scientific history, it has been shown that what our senses perceive as solid, may only *seem* to exist in the physical realm, but is really only non-solid energy.

If we really *are* only "frozen light" – energy – then what our body's eyes perceive as solid is only an illusion that we have created via our perception. Understanding this is the first step toward opening your mind to realizing what you see is not real. True reality lies within the unseen light spectrum that our eyes, and our senses cannot perceive.

The Meshing of "Knowing" and the Law of Attraction

At first it may seem strange or hard to comprehend how understanding that this life you are living is really an illusion, and that true reality lies within the unseen realm of infinite uncompromising love and Oneness (what I call "knowing"), has anything to do with the Law of Attraction. The explanation of their relationship will unfold throughout this book, but for now, let us establish their symbiosis.

In chapter one you learned the basics of how the Law of Attraction works, and in the next chapter we will cover the essentials of all the Universal laws, but now let's dig deeper into why it is important to "know" so you can live a joyous, happy, and abundant life – the life you truly desire to live.

Consistently manifesting the good, desired things into your life can only come about if you walk in harmony and resonance with your knowing and living the Universal Truths. Without doing so, sure you will sporadically and occasionally manifest your desires in conjunction with the Law of Attraction, but never consistently. Remember that since the L.O.A. is completely objective, it can only produce for you what you think and dwell upon with regularity. Because within the dream of this life that is ego-driven (duality), and you do not "know", only inconsistency in the creation of all the good things you desire can be the result. In its complete objectivity, the L.O.A. stays consistent by also delivering to you the bad, hurtful, and destructive things your thoughts and beliefs have been dwelling upon. (Some people are stuck in a habitually negative pattern of speech and thought and may never break out this cycle during their lifetime). Operating within the symbiotic relationship of Universal Eternal Truths and the Law of Attraction can consistently produce the good results you desire. However, what you say out loud with what you desire conflicts with what your heart says and derails its manifestation. *A Course in Miracles* addresses this.

"Let us suppose, then, that what you ask of the Holy Spirit is what you really want, but you are still afraid of it. Should this be the case, your attainment of it would no longer be what you want."

When the desires of your mind and heart conflict, it will always be what your heart is projecting that the Law of Attraction answers.

Perhaps one of the biggest criticisms about Law of Attraction practitioners is (as I once heard author, Gary Renard say), "It seems that the Law of Attraction is all about getting stuff!" I could see where this criticism comes from since the world mostly operates from only a materialistic, dualistic perspective. I'm sure there are far more L.O.A. practitioners who utilize it to get more stuff. The problem with this operational mode of using the L.O.A. is that it will never work *consistently*, and much of what the strictly materialistic user of the L.O.A. manifests will include the bad stuff along with the good. Even though Gary Renard understands how and why the L.O.A. works, he does have a valid point in stating that it's all about getting more stuff. Therefore, it is important to merge your personal belief, trust, and practice of living and walking in harmony with Universal Eternal Truths, and your practice of the Law of Attraction.

And why would God call our dream of separation from Him a "tiny mad idea"? If you think about it, it should be obvious as to why. God is infinite and All-That-Is, so within His view of our dream, it is simply a tiny error in the grand scheme of timeless infinity that within its reality was over in a moment. That moment being our concept of all that has and will ever exist within the Universe of space and time that we conjured up.

You've come this far with me, so I ask you to stick with me through the rest of this book, as we will teach you how to pull it all together into one cohesive, beautiful, loving, and joyful process of becoming a consistent co-creator with the Universe of all things good.

Chapter 4:

The Essential Universal Laws

"Universal Laws, also referred to as Spiritual Laws or Laws of Nature, are the unwavering and unchanging principles that rule our entire Universe and are the means by which our world continues to thrive and exist".

Christy Whitman, Law of Attraction teacher and coach

One thing that we need to do is gain clarity into understanding of just how to build a rock-solid personal foundation for yourself. This is important in-regards-to your mental, physical, and spiritual pillars, and based on operating in unison and harmony with eternal Universal truths and laws.

The very first thing we need to establish is that:

The Law of Attraction = Love

Now this may seem to be a gutsy statement, but when we look closer, and begin to understand on how this can be, it simply becomes an epiphany of sorts - A "but of course!" inherent understanding. Or, as Dr. Wayne Dyer calls it, a "Quantum Moment".

From the semi-mysterious writings and teachings of author Carlos Castaneda, comes, *"In the Universe there is an immeasurable, indescribable force which shamans call intent, and absolutely everything that exists in the entire cosmos is attached to intent by a connecting link."*

Greg Braaden's fascinating 2007 book, *The Divine Matrix*, states,

"While our precise role in creation is still not fully understood, experiments in the quantum realm clearly show that consciousness has direct effect on the most elementary particles of creation. And we are the source of the consciousness."

They call it intent, but I call it Love, if you will. But perhaps the most eye-opening statement regarding scientifically proven studies of the true nature of intent and Universal connectedness comes from Lynne McTaggert's book, *The Intention Experiment,*

"Intention appears to be something akin to a tuning fork, causing the tuning forks of other things in the universe to resonate at the same frequency."

The Law of Attraction has been called "the most powerful law in the universe" by many authors, researchers, and spiritual leaders. There is, as stated above in different ways, an undeniable, unbreakable, unseen interconnectedness of *everything*. Even though the label "Law of Attraction" may not always be used in their descriptions, but their words and definitions meet the criteria of "like attracts like", and "everything is energy".

A good example of this is Napoleon Hill's early 20th Century publication, *Think and Grow Rich.* His book was truly all about the Law of Attraction, although never once was the term used. This was because this "most powerful force in the Universe" had yet to gain this label, yet Hill's message within the book's pages is all about what we now call the Law of Attraction. As a matter of fact, Hill's first publisher deleted all usage of the word "vibration" (in his reference to all things being energy) from the original manuscript, because they thought the reading public wouldn't understand.

How then do I equate the Law of Attraction with being the same thing as Love? It goes back to the teachings and understanding that our oneness with our Source is based solely on the omniscient, never changing, eternal force of Love. Love *is* the Divine Matrix. Love *is* the connecting link. Love *is* Universal intent.

"Love is a sacred reserve of energy; it is like the blood of spiritual evolution".

Pierre Teilhard De Chardin

Since Love is the all-encompassing "All-That-Is", singular Universal Truth, and because the Law of Attraction is considered to be the most powerful law in the Universe, then it stands to reason that they are one-in-the-same.

Let us now take a look at some of the Universal Laws...

The 7 Essential Universal Laws

While teacher/author, Christy Whitman, may be one of the biggest proponents of these 7 Essential Universal Laws, they are by no means, new to the world. In some way, shape or form of thought and teaching, these laws are thought to be the basic building blocks of how you, me, we, each create our reality. The beauty of building your foundation, your life, based on these essential universal laws is that they are eternally unchanging. They will never, ever be affected by the ever-shifting sands of the continual change we perceive without question in our dualistic dream of this world. These universal laws are true – always! I highly encourage you to study and assess each of these Laws from an ego-less view, or a non-dualistic perspective. In doing so, you will stay in harmony and resonance with the Law of Love, of Oneness, of the *true* reality of the Creator of All-That-Is.

"Truth, which has no opposite, and cannot change".
- A Course in Miracles

Law #1: The Law of Attraction

This first law, the Law of Attraction, is the "umbrella" under which all other eternal, unchanging laws are encompassed. How can it not be when it is one with Love?

It is well worth it to again review just exactly what the Law of Attraction is:

- Where your attention goes, energy flows
- That which you focus your thoughts upon expands (Good or bad! This law is totally objective.)
- Like attracts like
- That which is like unto itself is drawn

Since you now understand that everything is energy, and that your thoughts are pure energy, you now start to get real careful on how you are focusing them. By *law*, the Law of Attraction *must* send more of what you are thinking and focusing upon, to you! Considering exactly how the Law of Attraction works, and exactly how everything in the Universe is connected, then you must consider the extensive universal implications of each and every one of your thoughts. If you are grounded in the dualistic reality of this life, then this consideration may seem like an almost unbearable responsibility, a heavy weight. However, if you let go of the dualistic dream of this world of lack, attack, limitations, thoughts of separation, and judgments, then realizing just how ultimately powerful each thought is, then it can be a totally freeing realization. Instead of being fearful of the power and ramifications of each of your thoughts, you can grasp their inherent infinite power to create and manifest by aligning them in perfect vibrational harmony and resonance with the Law of Attraction to create the life you truly desire.

Seemingly every self-improvement, "how to" book that is written these days offers a "simple formula", an "easy-to-do" process, and is literally mandated by editors and publishers because, "That is what the public wants! They don't have time to read anything long and involved. They have a problem, and issue and they want it fixed now!" Now I am not necessarily against that, and as a matter of fact this book will more than likely fulfill this "mandate" in many, many ways. What I do want you to understand when you close the back cover of this book after reading it is *you have the power to create your life exactly the way you truly desire it to be!* Better yet, understand that it is time for you to remember what you knew as a young child - you came here with this amazing pre-installed ability-to-create-power as you began your new life's journey. And it all starts here now upon remembering your Divine power to be, do and have whatever it is you desire. This epic power to create *anything* that you want gives you the freedom to be a deliberate co-creator with this all-encompassing, omniscient power called the Law of Attraction, and produces stunningly joyful, abundant, loving results. The Law of Attraction, in and of itself, will allow you to be a consistent happy creator as you stay in that very real non-dualistic realm of Oneness and knowing it is impossible for you to be separate from anything in the Universe. Remember, as you give, you receive.

One of the key things to remember when working with the Law of Attraction is...

The Power of Your Emotions

Now that you have remembered your pre-installed ability to manifest all that you desire, consider then one of the most powerful aspects to manifesting things into your life – your emotions.

As I like to tell people, this does not have to be complex. As a matter of fact, especially when it comes to utilizing and understanding the power of your emotions, it is very simple –

- If you feel good about what it is you wish to manifest, you are in energetic alignment with it.

- If you feel bad about what it is you wish to manifest, then you are not in energetic alignment with it.

And when you come to this realization of this simplicity, then you can truly start to implement practical utilization of the power of your emotions. Since everything is energy, including your thoughts, then as you add stronger and stronger emotion to what it is you desire to create, your emotions become amped-up energy that have grown in scope and power, and become, literally, as if you have thrown fuel on the fire. Your powerful emotions make the flames of your desire burn brighter, and shoot higher, and the Universe responds in kind by sending to you much quicker that which you desire.

In their book, *Ask & It is Given*, this is called your *Emotional Guidance System.*

As stated in this book by Abraham-Hicks,

"Your emotions are your indicators of the vibrational content of your Being, in every moment. And so, when you become aware of the feeling of your emotions, you can also be aware of your vibrational offering. And once you combine your knowledge of the Law of Attraction with your in-this-moment of what your vibrational offering is, then you will have full control of your own powerful point of attraction. With this knowledge, you can now guide your life experience in any way you choose."

Contemplating this amazing statement makes you realize just how truly powerful your emotions and thoughts are and how powerful *you* are. And once you have gained this knowledge and understanding of this, you truly can consistently co-create with the Universe.

And referring once again to the power of your emotions, Abraham-Hicks lists what they call the different degrees of your emotional guidance scale. They state that there are 22 different degrees of human emotion, starting at the bottom with the lowest being fear, and going to the top of the highest and most empowering being love.

You can see that humans are capable of quite a wide array of emotions, and no matter what level you are at from 1 to 22, as you resonate within that emotion, its powerful energy is attracting more of that emotion and all that goes with it into your life.

There are 6 more Essential Universal Laws, but before we look at law number two, I want you to remember that the Law of Attraction is *the* Universal Law. Once again...

Law of Attraction = Love

As we explore these six other Universal Laws, you will notice that they are simply extensions of the Law of Attraction, and that they have much interconnectedness and commonalities. It's all a part of the *Divine Matrix*, but they each have great value within their own right. Each Essential Universal Law is worthy of deep study, and utilization in consistently manifesting the things you truly desire to be in your life.

Law #2: The Law of Deliberate Creation:

As I noted in the section on the Law of Attraction because it is totally objective in aligning with your dominant thoughts, emotions, and energy, you can manifest things into your life by default. Having knowledge and understanding of this fact makes this second essential Universal Law, the Law of Deliberate Creation, a beautiful freeing thing. This is because you can now consciously direct your thoughts in the direction of the good, abundant, loving, happy, and joyful things you want to be in your life. And, yes, *now* you are no longer a "ship without a rudder", but a deliberate creator – you have the knowledge, you have the power, you understand you have the choice to point your stunningly powerful thoughts and desires in the direction of what you really want. This is yet another epiphany of freedom, and the realization that you can be and are a deliberate creator. The knowledge of your own inherent power to deliberately create drives home the understanding that you, only you, are the writer, director, and creator of your life – not your parents, not your employer, not your teacher, not your best friend – only you!

Once again, I would like to remind you of the power of your emotions when manifesting that which you desire. As with the Law of Attraction, so do your emotions amplify your intentions to create as you work hand-in-hand with the Law of Deliberate Creation. As the power of your feelings and emotions increase, direct them toward the abundant, happy, healthy, loving, beautiful, joyful things you want in your life.

One of my favorite affirmations applies perfectly here...

I am so grateful and happy that my thoughts are now in perfect harmony and resonance with all my highest right-minded aspirations, goals, dreams, and desires.

As always with using an affirmation, *repetition is key*. You may have opposing-subconscious thoughts. These thoughts can be slowly and surely overcome by constantly repeating the affirmation to your consciousness until it becomes accepted by your subconscious. Through your persistence in doing so, your subconscious adopts your affirmation as its norm.

Please note the underlining of the words "right-minded" as this is a very important differential. With your new understanding that the Law of Attraction is totally objective, you must remember that sometimes you may have aspirations and desires that dwell in the negative, destructive, self-defeating mode (much of the time subconsciously, driven by an entire lifetime of teaching of dualistic, ego-directed thought and belief system), so you must consciously direct your thoughts toward right-mindedness. Right-mindedness is your thought energy pointed toward a healthy, abundant, happy, loving, productive, and joyful place, so make sure your thoughts are focused in this direction so you can really become a happy co-creator with the Law of Deliberate Creation.

Affirmations and How To's:

- Declare your intentions
- Believe and feel your intentions and desires *already* exist
- Be grateful (thereby amplifying and magnifying your energetic vibrations you send out to the Universe)

- Expect success

- Stay focused on what you intend, not the absence of it. (As soon as you focus on it not yet being here, you become a creator by default)

- Take Inspired action to allow your desires to manifest

- Have faith and truly believe that the Universe is right now unfolding and orchestrating all that needs to happen for them to come to you – even though you can't see them yet.

- Release any and all thoughts that disallow, and are counterproductive to what you wish to manifest

- Trust the process, and remain detached from the outcome

Law #3: The Law of Allowing

Can it really be true that simply allowing what you want to manifest into your daily reality is one of the hardest things to do? Amazingly the answer is yes, and it all has to do with the fact that everything is energy and how you direct that power.

We've all been there, and way too many times – that is we want something so badly that we end up trying to force the Universe's hand to deliver it to us. Remember, in order for what you desire to manifest into your life, everything – the energy of your thoughts and desires, your emotions, and the energy of the Universe have to be in perfect alignment and resonance. When you want this thing so badly, you are trying to pound the proverbial square peg in a round hole. You are energetically setting up a roadblock to the manifestation of your desire by working in contrast to what should flow simply, easily, and effortlessly. This is tough to swallow when you want something so intensely, but that intensity is trying to energetically force the Law of Attraction's hand to deliver it the way you want it. Unfortunately, your idea of how your desire should manifest may not align with the Universe's idea of what is most beneficial to your overall good. This then becomes an energetic roadblock to its manifestation.

A good example of this is the time I was doing my daily run with a good friend of mine. As we ran, we were discussing how and what we like to have in our own lives, and her statement that, "I want what I want, what I want, and I want it now" really drove this concept home to me of wanting something so intensely. Needless to say, she could not understand why many of her desires were not showing up in her life.

How exactly do you overcome creating your own roadblock to the very thing you want to create? First take a deep breath and release the intensity of your desire. Now I don't mean give up on wanting it but let go of trying to force the hand of the Universe to make it happen. You have to trust; you have to have faith that your Source will send it to you. You don't have to do it all yourself. You don't have to do anything to make this thing you desire manifest into your life. You just need to *allow* it to happen, and this is based in your trust and faith that you are loved, cared for, and eternally supplied with everything you need and want by The Creator.

There is a beautiful quote from the children's animated movie, *The Rescuers* that really brings this point home...

Faith is a bluebird you see from afar.
It's for real and sure as the first evening star
You can't touch it or buy it or wrap it up tight
But it's there just the same
Making things turn out right.

Wanting what you want, and wanting it now, accompanied by your powerful emotional energy is a very strong energetic force. However, once again, this can get in the way of the ease and effortlessness of allowing it to manifest into form. When you put resistance under a microscope you can see that it really is fear, doubt, disappointment (Where's my stuff? I want it now!), lack, sadness, stress, and even anger. All of these are energy-draining emotions and thoughts.

When it comes to allowing true effortless and unblocked manifestation, I think we all have experienced some seemingly innocuous events of creation. One example is the manifesting of a parking spot. This example has been used many times (even in the movie, *The Secret*) You are going to the bank or the shopping mall, and you simply put the thought out there that, "I want a parking spot right in front of the building's door", and then you forget about it. Sure enough, upon arrival at your destination there is a parking spot right in front of the door like you asked for. This is one of the purest examples of easy and effortless manifestation, and not a meaningless coincidence. Effortless manifestation occurs when there is absolutely no powerful emotions or deeply hidden paradigms to block it.

I've already discussed the value of faith in allowing that which you desire to manifest, but on equal footing is trust. Trust really means being consistent – consistent in your faith and belief that the Universe really *is* working only for your highest good and aspirations. This places you in the flow of the pure, positive energy of the Law of Allowing.

Affirmations and How To's:

• Accept the moment

"You are not IN the universe, you ARE the universe, an intrinsic part of it. Ultimately you are not a person, but a focal point where the universe is becoming conscious of itself. What an amazing miracle." - Eckhart Tolle

- Take Responsibility for how you feel by using your free will to change how you feel.

- Choose to feel good!

- Practice defenselessness (This is where the faith and trust come in handy).

- Release, detach, and trust the process that your Creator always takes care of you, and supplies you with all that you need.

Law #4: The Law of Sufficiency & Abundance

This fourth Universal Law states that everything you could ever need or want is already yours, and simply awaits you asking for it. This is based on...

- The understanding that you are a Divine Being, a Spiritual Being who is having a human experience.

- The Universe contains an unlimited supply of every good and wonderful thing, and because your true self is at one with the Universe and your Divine Self, it is *all* available to you in every moment.

If this is true, then why is it most of us don't have all that we want right now? Speaking from personal experience, I realized that most of my thoughts and judgments of lack and unworthiness, etc. were based on un-truths. Since early childhood most of these un-truths have been pounded into our head from a multitude of sources, making us believe that it is impossible to have all that we want. This paradigm does not discriminate as it cuts across any and all socio-economic, race, and cultural lines. Those few individuals who do have all that they desire somehow managed to come to energetic resonance and alignment with the Law of Sufficiency and Abundance. They have literally escaped the invisible bindings that suppressed belief in the reality of their true desires.

A good place to start if you wish to activate and attract the energy of this law is gratitude. You first have to be grateful for what you do have and believe that you will always have enough. Also, remember that all seven of these Universal Laws are interconnected, so as you allow, focus on becoming a deliberate creator and understanding the principles of the workings of the Law of Attraction, then you are pointed in the right direction. If you are truly grateful for what you already have, the Universe must send you more to be grateful for. The icing on the cake lies within this Law of Sufficiency & Abundance in understanding that there is way more than enough for everyone! I think one of the most distinctive analogies regarding Universal unlimited abundance I ever heard was given by Dr. Wayne Dyer. He stated that if you drove a dump truck to the edge of the ocean and filled it with water, and continued to refill this truck with water over and over and over again, it would seem as if you had never taken a single drop, because the abundance of it is unlimited and eternal.

I have read and studied many definitions and interpretations of this essential Universal law, and here's the bottom line for me – *There has got to be a better way! There simply has got to be a better way than the millennia after millennia of the world's illusional and delusional ego-driven premise of lack!* Enough already of the illusion of there not being enough for everyone! And there *is* a better way, and that is knowing the truth – and I do mean the *truth* is – as the Child of God, at One with our Source, there is only an eternal flowing stream of well-being and abundance. How can it possibly be otherwise if we truly are One, where All-That-Is, *is*? In every moment, all that you could ever possibly want and need is available to you. It is time to rev-up your memory of being one with All-That-Is, that you have continuously buried under layer upon layer upon layer of your ego-forged self and forgotten about.

This is the truth about the essential Universal Law of Sufficiency & Abundance. As you pursue strengthening your personal mental, physical, and spiritual pillars, this remembering becomes more and more natural, and then the Law of Attraction sends more of what you are now remembering – more abundance.

Law #5: The Law of Pure Potentiality:

One of the core teachings that reoccur in all my writings is that the real truth is that we are a Divine Being at One with All-That-Is, and this falls directly in line with the fifth Essential Universal Law, The Law of Pure Potentiality. Almost every definition of this law that I have read point out that your true essence is that of pure consciousness. Reading this statement may be kind of scary for you, especially if you are deeply invested in believing that your body is the be-all-do-all, end of everything. When you take this perspective, you are limiting your potentiality in many, many different ways. Understanding that your true essence is pure consciousness can offer you a huge sense of relief and freedom, because it literally lifts the heavy shackles of the limits of your body, expands your vision of what is possible, and inspires you to take action in the direction of what you previously thought was impossible. The Law of Pure Potentiality also validates my personal mantra that "*Ordinary people can accomplish extraordinary things*". When you are in alignment with the potential of creating your dreams, goals, and aspirations, then you really can release your extraordinary from deep within you.

The Law of Pure Potentiality is the one Universal Law that can really blow your mind, because it is so essentially metaphysical. The ego-based world that identifies with a body as the only reality, simply cannot relate to anything metaphysical. So here we are now faced with a Universal Law that says you are not really a body, and that you are not separate from the person sitting next to you or the person on the other side of the world. It says that because you are pure consciousness and pure energy, and there can be no separation of anything or anyone, all is connected and potentially anything and everything is available to you in every moment. Since you are pure consciousness within the field of pure potentiality, this leads to Self-Power.

Here's what inspirational guru, Deepak Chopra has to say about Self-Power and the Law of Pure Potentiality, "*It draws people to you, and it also draws things that you want to you. It magnetizes people, situations, and circumstances to support your desires. This is also called support from the laws of nature. It is the support of divinity; it is the support that comes from being in the state of grace. Your power is such that you enjoy a bond with people, and people enjoy a bond with you. Your power is that of bonding-a bonding that comes from true love*".

As attractive and exciting as this concept of pure potentiality is, it takes a powerful trust to take the leap of faith to believe and practice this Universal Law.

Chopra offers even more insight into just how to access the power of pure potentiality, "*How can we apply the Law of Pure Potentiality, the field of all possibilities, to our lives? If you want to enjoy the benefits of the field of pure potentiality, if you want to make full use of the creativity which is inherent in pure consciousness, then you have to have access to it. One way to access the field is through the daily practice of silence, meditation, and non-judgment. Spending time in nature will also give you access to the qualities inherent in the field: infinite creativity, freedom, and bliss.*"

What makes pure potentiality seem so foreign to most people on the planet is that they don't practice silence, meditation, and non-judgment. Heck, billions of people live in huge metropolitan areas with virtually no nature to commune with and enjoy. I am not trying to be a naysayer here, but instead I'm here to point out to you that now you have the knowledge of what it takes to tap into pure potentiality. Now the knowledge of this law is allowing your understanding of the power to create and manifest what it is that you want to filter into your mind and heart. It really doesn't matter if you have no access to nature, or even some quiet time, because you have the inherent, built-in personal power to tap into your oneness with the Universe via your desire and intention to do so. Still, seek the quiet when the opportunity arises.

Law #5 How To's:

- Talk to your Source in genuine prayer and meditation, and ask for what you want.

- Listen to your Source in stillness and quiet for the answers.

- Act, think, and speak in alignment with the eternal truth of Love and Oneness, which resonates beautifully with the sufficiency and abundance you desire.

- Always practice non-judgment.

Law #6: The Law of Detachment –

Let's start with this poignant, but simple formula...

ATTACHMENT = RESISTANCE

Let's take a look at one of my personal experiences of wanting something so badly, and not being able to detach from the outcome. This is a topic that I am sure many of you can relate to – romantic relationships.

There was a lovely young, beautiful woman that I was madly head-over-heels in love with. Being a guy, (and guys tend to mature much slower than women), I kept pushing and pushing for our relationship to go to a more serious place, and not only did I start pushing her away, I became jealous, too. The more I pushed for her to come closer to me romantically, the more I pushed her away. I know this is not an uncommon story, but it is my story of not being mature enough to know that I needed to detach myself from the situation. Yes, "I want what I want what I want, and I want it now"! As stated earlier, this kind of energy only creates blockages to allow the Universe to do its effortless work of delivering that which you desire. Unfortunately, it was way too late before I learned the lesson of detaching from the outcome, and I lost her in my life (we did, however, end up being great friends, which is a testimonial to what a wonderful heart she has).

Once you decide to master The Law of Detachment, you enter into the exciting realm of uncertainty. When you enter into this dimension of uncertainty as you attempt to manifest what you desire, you must detach your emotions from it and enter into an agreement of trust and faith in the Universe's capable hands to deliver it to you. Unfortunately for most of us, this is not an easy thing to do. In fact, of all the 7 Essential Universal Laws, this one is considered by many to be the hardest of all to align with. The statement, "I want what I want what I want, and I want it now" is an excellent example of the power of your emotions. However, in this case, it is a powerful negative energy of resistance. When you want something so badly, you literally are trying to force the hand of the Universe to deliver it to you, and as you may have already begun to see, this is not how it works. In fact, it *doesn't* work! When you detach yourself from the outcome, utilizing your very real trust and faith, then you have created the freedom for the Universe to not only deliver to you that which you desire, but perhaps something even better.

As Deepak Chopra states,

"Through the wisdom of uncertainty, I will find my security."

I know this sounds contradictory to what we're taught to believe (in *certainty* comes security), but as you step into this newfound freedom of detaching from the outcome of how, when, and where your desire will come to you, you gradually start to understand a key factor. That is, you have to practice non-judgment and defenselessness. This also includes allowing the people and things around you to be who and what they are meant to be without you trying to force them to change or be what you think they should be. In freeing them from your judgment, this allows the natural flow of the Universe to work effortlessly and joyously without your "forced" energy blocking the way. *This* is trust in All-That-Is to orchestrate and align all that is needed to allow your desires to manifest in perfect timing. This is *true* detachment. This is detachment based on abundance consciousness backed by trust and faith.

Law #6 How To's:

- Know that the Universe may deliver to you what you want in a form that may not seem like what you asked for but is disguised in a form beneficial to your greatest good.

- Learn to take the necessary inspired action and move on. The results will take care of themselves.

- Trust in the Universe's ability to deliver that which you desire, and things will manifest in perfect timing.

- If you lack trust in the Universe to do its job, you create blockages through lack of trust, doubt, insecurities, and fear, so let go and let God.

The bottom line is that when you are in alignment with the Law of Detachment, you don't force things to happen, you simply allow them to come or not come to you (at least in the form and timeline you imagined). If what you desire does not show up, then know that the deep subconscious paradigms of your mind and heart that may be in opposition of what you asked for were energetically much stronger than your verbal asking. When you allow, you are then in vibrational alignment with the pure positive energy of the Universe, and things seemingly flow magically and effortlessly to you.

LAW #7: THE LAW OF POLARITY:

You live in a dualistic framework that you perceive as your life here on planet earth. While I have pointed out before that many religions and metaphysical teachings say that this dualistic life is simply an illusion that keeps us separate from our true oneness with The Creator, it doesn't negate the fact that you are here within this body and life (be it an illusion or not), and you have to deal with it. In order to deal with it, you have to have a good working understanding of the seventh essential Universal law, The Law of Polarity.

Two Ends of a Stick

There are many, many ways in which to explain this law, but one of the simplest is to use the analogy of a stick. Obviously, a stick has two ends to it. You can't have the one end without the other. Of course, this is true in any situation, thing, place, time, etc. The classic examples are hot and cold, love and fear, dark and light. What I find very important to note is that when one is present, its opposite disappears. One does not exist in the presence of the other. In other words, try as you might, you cannot have both at the same time. With *A Course in Miracles* being one of the human race's main sources of right-minded guidance, we once again turn to it to become consistent, loving, productive, positive co-creators with the Universe.

"Whatever is true is eternal and cannot change or be changed. Spirit is therefore unalterable because it is already perfect, but the mind can elect what it chooses to serve. The only limit put on its choice is that it cannot serve two masters. If it elects to do so, the mind can become the medium by which spirit creates along the line of its own creation".

This is beautiful to contemplate if you are serious about becoming a consistent co-creator with the Universe to manifest the things in your life that you really want. Now, with your understanding of how the Law of Polarity works, you can direct your choices between the two opposites, and build your rock-solid foundation. You must remember, however, that your choice and perception play a key role in this process.

I love how Law of Attraction teacher, speaker, and author, Bob Proctor, references how you can use the Law of Polarity...

"Realize that every situation JUST IS; you make it negative or positive by virtue of how you choose to think about the situation. When you look at the situation one way and it is negative, you can change your perspective and look at it from the opposite viewpoint and find, it will be positive".

As you can see that by utilizing your choice, guided by right-mindedness, allows you to make decisions that will empower your life to be more productive, happier, abundant, and even healthier. *This* is making use of the Law of Polarity in a way to build the path to the life you desire. But remember, *you cannot serve two masters*!

One of the most important things to remember as you study, learn, and live with these seven essential Universal laws is using them intelligently within the realm of the dream of your life, to live well and joyously. But don't get hung up on them without remembering the spiritual truth that helps your personal foundation and 3 Pillars stay rock-solid!

Lesson 152 in the A.C.I.M. succinctly states, "*...the truth is true and nothing else is true...Truth cannot have an opposite. This cannot be too often said and thought about. For if what is not true is true as well as what is true, then part of truth must be false. And truth has lost its meaning. Nothing but the truth is true, and what is false is false.*"

This flies directly in the face of what the Law of Polarity states – that everything has an opposite! However, this doesn't mean that you can't use an understanding of this law to live and maintain your life within your dualistic perspective here on earth. But remembering that "*...the truth is true and nothing* *else is true"* will always stabilize and strengthen your house - your life, to stand strong for the ages. Remembering and practicing this will work wonders in times of stress and conflict that threatens to destabilize your 3 Pillars.

The whole point to my covering the 7 Essential Universal Laws comes to this, and that is utilizing them to make the right-minded choices necessary to make the 3 Pillars of your personal foundation stand for the ages and not suffer from constantly choosing the wrong end of the stick.

Law #7 How To's:

- Understand that you can focus on and choose the opposite of what you don't want (the bad or un-wanted) to what you do want (the good or wanted). The choice is yours!

- By focusing on what you don't want, you create resistance to the manifestation of what you do want, so accept and be grateful for everything as it is, and you become the polar opposite of resistance.

Chapter 5:

Worldwide Enlightenment

"The truth is that enlightenment is neither remote nor unattainable. It is closer than your skin and more immediate than your next breath. If we wonder why so few seem able to find that which can never be lost, we might recall the child who was looking in the light for a coin he dropped in the dark because 'the light is better over here' ".

Jed McKenna from his book "Spiritual Enlightenment: The Damnedest Thing"

I grew up in working class home in Cleveland, Ohio in the post-World War II era of the '50's and '60's. Born to a mother, Anne Gacnik, of Slovenian heritage, who was born without 9 of her 10 fingers and only nubs for toes (yet played piano, drove, knit and raised two rambunctious boys), and Henry Gruber, a corporal in the U.S. Army. Hank fought in the in the infamous Battle of the Bulge as a gunner in a Sherman tank and became a life-long factory worker. For many decades I had no clue on how fortunate I was to have parents like Hank and Anne who, as I realized in hindsight, never forced their beliefs and opinions down my brother's or my throats. We never went to church, and had no religious affiliation, although I knew that my mother had quit the Catholic church when she was 19 years old. Rarely, if ever, was religion or the topic of God even mentioned or spoken about in our home. What I came to finally realize is this – this lack of religious dogma, or even any religious training left my adolescent and adult mind a clean slate for my own future absorption of spiritual teachings.

Once I got into my late teens and early 20's, I started to become more inquisitive when I brushed against the topic of religion, God, and any form of spirituality. My "clean slate" just kind of absorbed this information via osmosis from my Catholic friends – only I didn't get hooked on the religious dogma. Instead, I gravitated to the deeper meaning of it all – the God part and wanted to know how I was a part of it, and how it was a part of me.

Fast forward a few decades, and I found myself still with my ever-present sense of "there has to be something better than this" propelling me to go toward the Light. This, of course, now applies to all of humanity, as I have simply been a part of the long, slow awakening to the truth of our Oneness with All-That-Is. My spiritual awakening, and the remembering of the Divinity of my true self has been a long, slow evolution of learning. Beginning with the writings and teachings of the Father of Positive Thinking, Dr. Norman Vincent Peale, author of the best-seller, *The Power of Positive Thinking,* I then gravitated to Dr. Robert Schuller, Anthony Robbins, Napoleon Hill, Dr. Wayne Dyer, Deepak Chopra, etc. Through my studies of these powerful teachings of awakening to our own inherent power and understanding that our Source is that of pure light, love, and truth, I have since called myself a student of Positive, Possibility, Power Thinking.

The Next Step

I was totally stoked about my Positive, Possibility, Power Thinking personal philosophy (as fueled by the multiple conveyors of The 3P's). Little did I know just how much more enlightenment awaited/awaits me, as I stumbled upon (actually I was Divinely directed, but it seemed like hap stance) a book of pure Light and Love called, *A Course in Miracles.*

A Course in Miracles is a very unique, one-of-a-kind publication that is a dictated text and written down by Helen Schucmann, a teacher at Columbia University in New York City. It is written in the voice of Jesus, but is in no way, shape, or form a document of religious dogma. Instead, it is a concise, to-the-point instruction of the pure light, love, and truth of our *real* existence, and has at times been described as a "Christian Vedanta."

For a description of how the *A.C.I.M.* came into being, I turn directly to a quote from the publisher's (The Foundation for Inner Peace) website...

Helen Schucman, Ph.D., was a clinical and research psychologist, who held the tenured position of Associate Professor of Medical Psychology at the College of Physicians and Surgeons at the Columbia-Presbyterian Medical Center in New York City. ***A Course in Miracles*** was "scribed" by Dr. Schucman between 1965 and 1972 through a process of inner dictation. She experienced the process as one of a distinct and clear dictation from an inner voice, which earlier had identified itself to her as Jesus. Helen Schucman's scribing of ***A Course in Miracles*** began with these words: *"This is a course in miracles, please take notes."*

They say that the teacher will show up when the student is ready. Evidently, I was not ready immediately, even though *A Course in Miracles* showed up in my life.

The very first time I ever heard of the *A.C.I.M.* was from the mouth of Dr. Wayne Dyer, who mentioned it in an interview he was doing with Anthony

Robbins. It was 2002, and I went to the local bookstore, purchased it, and then proceeded to let it sit on my shelf for two years without even opening the front cover. When I was finally ready to start studying it in 2004, I (like so many) had a very difficult time comprehending the wording and teaching the *A.C.I.M.* offers. This is because the teaching is such a radical departure from the ego-based, dualistic learning system that has been hard-wired into our DNA from the moment we were born, but substantial portions of it are written in the rhythm of iambic pentameter, the same literary style as that of Shakespeare. Not having ever been a huge reader of Shakespeare, it was only through daily repetition and persistence that I was finally able to start to absorb and learn some of the teachings of the Universal Truth of our own Divinity and the real Truth of our Oneness.

So, the stage was set for me to receive the message of truth of our Divine creation and reality, of who we *really* are – spirit having an extended dream of the human experience. That may be true for me, but how is it now playing out on the global population platform?

While *A Course in Miracles* was the demarcation point in time in the 20th. Century as a primer in launching the modern mind into an awakening enlightenment of the truth, the advent of another form of media in the early 21st. century occurred to further expand thoughts and understanding of the most powerful law in the Universe – the Law of Attraction.

The timing could not have been better in 2006 for an Australian named Rhonda Byrne, to conceive of and produce the movie, *The Secret*. Aptly titled, *The Secret* proceeded to explain that the idea of and the concept of the Law of Attraction that had been mostly kept a secret throughout all of history. It was used by the intelligentsia and the rich and powerful to keep the masses under their thumb and rule. Although the understanding of the L.O.A., had been written about and discussed via many different forums throughout history (i.e., "Think and Grow Rich" by Napoleon Hill), it was still unknown by the vast majority of the world's population up until this point in time.

This movie turned into a global phenomenon that virtually exploded the word about this powerful law – of being able to actually manifest what you want through your own thought, focus, energy, and intention – and greatly contributed to it no longer being a secret. As I stated, the timing of the movie's release was tuned perfectly with the exponential rise in technology via the internet, communication devices, that allowed for *The Secret* to race at light speed to the masses. This "lightning quick" spread about not just the Law of Attraction, but spiritual enlightenment may still seem at times to be moving at a snail's pace, but surely forward – after all the world's population now exceeds 7 billion (at the time of this writing). However, the global spiritual awakening continues to expand consistently and assuredly. This of course, recalls the famous line, "Nothing is more powerful than an idea whose time has come!"

What exactly is the current status of global-wide spiritual enlightenment, and where do we go from here? Jeff Warren's article in the November 2012 issue of *Psychology Tomorrow*, says a mouthful –

"For expediency's sake, I'll define enlightenment as a complex and multi-faceted process by which the mind comes to know – and over time rest more securely in – its own ground. As this happens, our habitual sense of being a separate and bounded self begins to fade. Ultimately, the person for whom this happens no longer feels themselves to be an autonomous entity looking out at an external world; rather, they feel themselves, more and more, to be an intimate part of that world's humid expression, an unfolding natural process no different than anything else in nature. As a result, practitioners report a liberating sense of freedom, ease, spontaneity. The volume of self-referential thought often decreases, although, since enlightenment happens along a deepening continuum, they are still routinely trapped in old habits of dualistic thinking.

Despite the fact that this transformation has been painstakingly described in virtually every contemplative tradition – from Buddhism, Taoism and Hinduism through to the mystical branches of the Western Abrahamic religions – and is the central drama in the lives of thousands of lucid and intelligent human beings, here in the West there is zero mention of the phenomenon in any of our bastions of intellectual respectability. You'll never read about spiritual enlightenment in a Malcolm Gladwell book, or the pages of The New York Review of Books. This is true even in most Western Buddhist books, where enlightenment may be mentioned as a general principle or orientation, but almost never as a tangible transformation that happens to real 21st-century human beings."

This is most definitely not your father's religion, plus it is not even religion. That is something that needs to be made perfectly clear – spiritual enlightenment is *not* religion! This is about awakening to the deeper understanding hidden in the deeper strata of your mind of your true nature and natural connectedness to the eternal, unchanging Universal Truths. These Truths cannot be nor ever will be subject to the ever-shifting sands of the world's ego-driven perspective of disconnect and belief of being completely separated from our Creator.

As Jeff Warren so eloquently points out, *"There is a new spirit of openness, for instance, in both the culture of spirituality and the culture of science. One spiritual Trojan horse is yoga. Another is the increasingly popular practice of "mindfulness." Both of these are powerful spiritual technologies. Most people approach them for practical fitness or stress-reduction reasons, and this is all they ever deliver on. But, for a small percentage, something else happens. They find themselves – deliciously, inexorably, sometimes alarmingly – moving along a course of spiritual development they never expected."*

Religion or Spirituality?

Considering this worldwide, slowly but surely spreading epiphany of spiritual enlightenment, the question arises, is there any evidence of this? The evidence would seem to be coming in the form of large portions of the global population eschewing formal religious practices and adherence for the more freeing option of simply being spiritual. Basically, being spiritual is having a belief that there is a greater power, One Source of All-That-Is, and pursuing the knowledge of the eternal Universal Laws of Love and Oneness. And the evidence is slowly starting to appear as author, writer, publisher, D. Patrick Miller explains in his 2016 eBook, "*The Rapid Dying of Religion: And the Rise of a Universal Spirituality*",

"The latest evidence of the dying of organized religion issues from a large survey released in 2014 by the Pew Research Center. Among the findings of their Religious Landscape Study was this information, as reported by Michael Lipka:

"Religious 'nones' – a shorthand we use to refer to people who self-identify as atheists or agnostics, as well as those who say their religion is 'nothing in particular' – now make up roughly 23% of the U.S. adult population. This is a stark increase from 2007, the last time a similar Pew Research study was conducted, when 16% of Americans were 'nones.' (During this same time period, Christians have fallen from 78% to 71%.)"

If this rate of "conversion" to religious nonehood should continue, with a one-percent annual increase, then over half of the US population will be religiously unaffiliated in less than thirty years — and the proportion of Christians will likewise fall below 50%. In all likelihood, however, the rate of change to non-religiosity is likely to accelerate, because the bulk of current churchgoers is aging out of circulation while younger "Millennials" are staying away from church in droves. Thirty-five percent of those born from 1981 to 1996 identify themselves as "nones," and earlier polls have indicated that around 70% of Millennials identify themselves as SBNR."

And according to Miller, there are multiple reasons to sight for this movement toward spiritual enlightenment, one of them being...

"A release of guilt and the belief in "original sin" in favor of advanced self-awareness and transcendent forgiveness. Traditional Christianity identifies human beings as sinful by nature, and redeemable only by accepting the grace of Jesus Christ as one's "personal savior." By contrast, modern spiritual paths dispense with the idea of original sin in favor of admitting that while human beings are generally flawed and prone to making mistakes (sometimes very serious ones), their only "salvation"

lies in learning to become more self-aware, responsible, and consistently forgiving. In A Course in Miracles (ACIM), by far the most popular SBNR discipline with recent Western roots, forgiveness is in fact the paramount value, expressed in such meditative lessons as "Forgiveness ends all suffering and loss" and "Fear binds the world. Forgiveness sets it free."

While I may have missed the part of being indoctrinated into a specific religious dogma, my individual journey has followed the path of the many seeking a kinder, softer, more loving, coming-to-know-who-I-really-am spirituality. And the forgiveness that Miller speaks of strikes a chord within me, especially as I have delved deeper into the teaching of A Course in Miracles. As you will see as this treatise develops and expands over these many pages, I unfold the concept of Quantum Forgiveness – a Divine form of forgiveness heretofore unknown and un-understood by humankind.

Just where is this "worldwide enlightenment" going, and just how can each of us utilize it to create a sane, loving, peaceful world based in the right-mindedness of spiritual enlightenment? Basically, the fading away of religion in the world's populace, and the continual rise of individual spiritual awakening (or, Spiritual But Not Religious), is creating a blank canvas for future generations in which to blossom their enlightenment. This "blank canvas" means that people can now learn, absorb, and integrate it into their own lives without any interference from the lies and falsehoods organized religion has used throughout history to control the people, and solidify the power and wealth of those in charge. There is no conflict, and this allows you to shed any thoughts of guilt, unworthiness, and lack, but instead to creatively and perfectly paint the canvass of their own mind based on the Universal Truth of Love and Oneness. According to A Course in Miracles, this is the only reality, the only truth.

As further evidence of the movement toward becoming S.B.N.R., one of the most telling events about the direction that organized religion is going came in a 2006 interview by Keith Morrison on Dateline ABC news with retired Episcopal Bishop, John Shelby Spong. He stated that...

Spong: *I don't think Hell exists. I happen to believe in life after death, but I don't think it's got a thing to do with reward and punishment. Religion is always in the control business, and that's something people don't really understand. It's in a guilt-producing control business. And if you have Heaven as a place where you're rewarded for you goodness, and Hell is a place where you're punished for your evil, then you sort of have control of the population. And so they create this fiery place, which has quite literally scared the Hell out of a lot of people, throughout Christian history. And it's part of a control tactic.*

Morrison: *But wait a minute. You're saying that Hell, the idea of a place under the earth or somewhere you're tormented for an eternity – is actually an invention of the church?*

Spong: *I think the church fired its furnaces hotter than anybody else. But I think there's a sense in most religious life of reward and punishment in some form. The church doesn't like for people to grow up, because you can't control grown-ups. That's why we talk about being born again. When you're born again, you're still a child. People don't need to be born again. They need to grow up. They need to accept their responsibility for themselves and the world.*

If this had been stated by *anyone* a few centuries ago (maybe not even that long ago!), Mr. Spong would have been labeled as a heretic, and put to death! Now, in this open era of spiritual growth, not only does this bishop have the freedom to express this opinion, but his words are a welcome "growing up" of the people of the world who openly, and gladly state, "I'm Spiritual, but not religious!"

As one of the people who have a "blank canvas" ready to absorb the *real* truth of my own pre-installed Divine power to create the world I wish to see and live in, and walking in the integrity of right-mindedness of Oneness and Love, I welcome more people like John Shelby Spong to help allow the truth and the light to dawn upon the minds of all who are ready to receive it.

Chapter 6:

Mindfulness & Right-Mindedness

The terms "mindfulness" and "right-mindedness" are two very important factors to be carefully considered and studied when moving forward with your desire of achieving spiritual awakening. They are also integrally important as key elements when building your rock-solid personal foundation supported by your 3 Pillars.

On the surface, these two terms seem almost indistinguishable in definition, but upon our closer investigation, we will discover what their primary differences are, and how you can utilize both to further enhance your life – your foundation.

Mindfulness:

From Wikipedia...

Mindfulness involves intentionally bringing one's attention to the internal and external experiences occurring in the present moment. It can be developed through the practice of meditation, which can be defined as the intentional self-regulation of attention from moment to moment. Meditative practices in the Buddhist tradition are a popular way to develop the practice of meditation. The Five-Aggregate Model, an ancient link between mind and body, is a helpful theoretical resource that can guide mindfulness interventions. The term "mindfulness" is derived from the Pali-term sati, which is an essential element of Buddhist practice. The modern movement of mindfulness was appropriated from ancient Buddhist roots.

As you can see from this definition, mindfulness has ancient roots and can just as easily be called meditation. The curious thing about the fact that mindfulness has ancient roots, yet it is *the* politically correct modern term to use instead of the word "meditation." (Notice that the above definition states that mindfulness can be developed through meditation. There is total meditation/mindfulness interconnectedness from its conception) For example, I have a friend who is a counselor in a high school who has convinced not only the school's administrators, but also the student body, to have a "Morning Mindfulness Minute" before classes start for the day. He explained that if he were to have used the word "meditation", the idea would have been turned down, and the student's parents would be in an uproar that the school was teaching their kids "mumbo-jumbo."

Here is yet another perspective (from Tim Lomas, Phd., in *Psychology Today* on-line) of just how nuanced the word mindfulness can be...

"I feel I do get a sense of what sati refers to. But then, the question arises, why was 'mindfulness' picked as a translation for sati? The term mindfulness was first coined by the great Buddhist scholar T. W. Rhys Davids at the dawn of the 20th Century. Interestingly though, Rhys Davids toyed with various terms before settling on mindfulness. In his 1881 publication of Buddhist suttas, sati was rendered as 'mental activity,' and even simply as 'thought.' It was then only with his 1910 work that he settled on the term mindfulness. The word was then later picked up and embraced by Jon Kabat-Zinn when he formulated his Mindfulness-Based Stress Reduction programme, which was so influential in bringing mindfulness to the West. And, he does indeed seem to capture the 'flavour' of sati in his influential 2003 definition of mindfulness – which he explicitly stated was based upon sati –

namely 'the awareness that arises through paying attention on purpose, in the present moment, and nonjudgmentally to the unfolding of experience moment by moment.'"

Not only is this a lesson in semantics, but also the strange state of the general modern American attitude of anything considered metaphysical. Yet this is a tiny example of how an easy-to-use form of self-enlightenment is quietly making inroads to the global personal and spiritual awakening movement – and successfully so, as we have seen from verifiable statistics. However, whether it is politically correct to use the word "mindfulness", thereby causing less social consternation, or not, then so be it. *Whatever* the word be that brings you closer to the understanding and the truth of your real Self and not an illusion of the false, separated self that you have been scammed by the ego into believing you are, then use that word, that thought, that energy, with consistency. Consistent mindfulness leads to consistent right-mindedness, as we shall see.

Right-Mindedness:

Taking the cue from the last sentence, "Consistent mindfulness leads to consistent right-mindedness," let us now delve into the topic of right-mindedness.

Right-mindedness is not a term that you will see or hear on a daily basis. It is, however, one of the more important terms that you will ever incorporate into your daily life as you seek to build your rock-solid personal foundation. As the world holds its view of right-mindedness, it supposedly is about living your life morally, and abstaining from the worldly to obtain the other worldly. The Hindu perspective of right-mindedness can range anywhere from renunciation of certain things and actions (sacrifice) to freedom from cruelty and lust.

A Course in Miracles succinctly states that right-mindedness, *"The Holy Spirit is nothing more than your right mind."*

What this means is that when you are in the state of right-mindedness, you are in your natural state of Oneness with God. Anything else that is not in this perfect state of synchrony with God is wrong mindedness. It is part of the illusion of separation from Source. Knowing if you are speaking, thinking, or acting in either right or wrong-mindedness is exactly like my previous example of paying attention to your emotions – if you feel good about what you are doing, then you *are* in alignment with your desires. If you feel bad about what you are doing, then you are not in alignment with what you desire. With this consideration, right-mindedness means you *are*, and wrong mindedness means you are not.

And here's the wonderful thing about all of this, right-mindedness is your true natural state. You intuitively *know* you are on the right path once you start walking in right-mindedness. With your correct choice for right-mindedness, there is a natural flow of peace and tranquility. If you've chosen the path of wrong mindedness to walk, you will know that you've chosen poorly because this path is always marked by guilt, frustration, anger, and any and all negative emotions and energies.

A quick look at the dictionary's definition of "right-mindedness" states,
: having a right or honest mind
a right-minded citizen
right-mindedness
noun

The problem with this definition is that it is based in the dualistic, judgmental thought system of the ego's world, which is where we reside in this dream life, and what we are trying to leave behind. Non-dualistic right-mindedness is not based on egotistical judgment, but in the pure enlightenment of eternal Universal Truth of Oneness and Love.

Right-Mindedness: An Essential Building Block

Now that you have a better grasp of just what right-mindedness is you can now move forward in integrating its characteristics – its truths, into your daily thoughts and actions. Doing so is one of the essentials in creating and solidifying that rock solid personal foundation that I keep speaking about.

Whether you establish right-mindedness via meditation or mindfulness, the important part is that in doing so you establish integrity. As is so evident on a moment-to-moment basis in your daily comings and goings, integrity seems to be somewhat of a rare commodity amongst your fellow humans. The type of integrity that I am speaking about here, based in your now established right-mindedness, blossoms out of your alignment with the principles and truth of All-That-Is. In the true reality of All-That-Is, there is no conflict, no change, no evil, no lack, no darkness. Instead, you walk through your life in full light, love, truth, and expansion. When you accomplish this, it actually is impossible to not have integrity, because you live your life in perfect harmony with spiritual truth, and spiritual truth is true reality, not the illusory world where you believe you are separate from everyone and everything.

When you consistently walk in the integrity of right-mindedness, there is a natural understanding on your part that you are always taken care of and that you are one with All-That-Is. Consequently, you can walk upright and confident in the realization that there no longer is any reason for you to think of or perform any attack or judgment. Feelings of lack and vulnerability simply melt away. *This* is true right-minded integrity, and once you achieve it and establish it within yourself, you soon come to realize that now you really have laid down one of the biggest foundational stones of your whole being. Once you have accomplished this then you are well on your way to becoming a consistent co-creator with the Universe in manifesting the life you truly desire to live.

With this unmovable, rock-solid foundational stone of right-minded integrity holding up your "house", there is no longer even the need to consider or worry about your life crashing in on you. In a world that bases its reality on all that is negative, consistently shifting and changing and deteriorating, finding your right-minded integrity is a beautiful, freeing thing. I can guarantee that there will be a lightness in your step that you had never noticed before, and as if a very heavy weight has been lifted off your shoulders.

I want you to know, I mean really *know*, that building, establishing, and keeping a rock-solid foundation of right-minded integrity is *not* impossible. And, considering the world's view and perception of life, it is a downright miracle. However, remember that the very first line on page one of *A Course in Miracles* states...

"There is no order of difficulty in miracles."

If you don't feel like you are there just yet in establishing right-minded integrity in your life, don't worry because it is infinitely patient. It waits for you to find it in your own way, in your own time, and when you are ready to receive it. But if you are constantly in a dark place, with the ever-shifting landscapes of life seeming like quicksand to you, then perhaps it's time for you to make an active search to find this key element called right-minded integrity. Such writings as this one is a good place to begin.

The World Is Insane

The classic quote on the topic of insanity is, *"If one keeps doing what they've always done expecting different results, one will keep getting the same results they've always gotten."*

In a recent podcast interview that I did with author of the book, *The Supernatural Power of Thought*, James Goi, Jr., he stated that the majority of the world's population qualifies as being insane. This may seem like a gutsy statement, because (again) most people have an ego-based perception of the world – that is that true reality is one of judgment, lack, attack, ever-changing, and ever-shifting, and that eventually everyone and everything that lives will deteriorate and die. Because of this "insanity" the foundation of the world is constantly crumbling and fallen in on itself and imploding. There is no right-minded integrity to hold up the world's house!

I don't know about you, but I simply am not willing to live my life, nor see anyone else live their life in an insane world. It doesn't have to be, nor does it ever again have to be an insane, ego-driven world. The knowledge, the teaching, the understanding, the love – *the Truth* – is waiting for you and each person on the planet to take a hold of it and permanently implement it into the structure of their being.

Now to me, *this* is exciting, and it should be exciting for you knowing that you too can have and keep right-minded integrity – *now.*

I am always talking about just how key to creating a strong personal foundation for your life involves laying down some strong building blocks to your very being. With this in mind, let's once again turn to author, James Goi, Jr. and a quote from his book, "*The Supernatural Power of Thought,*

"You can think. Thought has power. The supernatural power of thought is your power. Before now, your thoughts have been relatively ineffective and unproductive compared to what they could be. The new you and your new life will spring forth from thought. All the other elements for creating the new you and your new life will spring forth from thought as well. To remind you, those other elements are feeling, intention, planning, envisioning, contemplation, understanding, work, and exercising free will...And there you have them, the building blocks."

And know *you* have it, as the power of your own thoughts, are the key to creating those rock-solid building blocks; to creating your right-minded integrity. You do so by exercising your own free will to make that key change within your being. No longer will you be a part of the insane thinking and perception of the world as you now understand that you get different results by doing and thinking in a new positive, productive way to achieve different results.

Chapter 7

TRUE SPIRITUALITY & THE LAW OF ATTRACTION: A Beautiful Symbiotic Relationship

My personal journey with what many have named as the greatest law in the Universe, the Law of Attraction, has been a wonderful years-long one of the opening up of my heart and mind. This journey has been an expansion of my ego-filled self who could not see beyond nor understand why the world is nothing but continual chaos, war, insanity, and ever changing. The only seeming constant in this world is that everything eventually deteriorates and dies. In my own mind's eye, I have always been a happy-go-lucky guy who had the ability to let criticism, problems, and roadblocks just kind of roll off me like water rolls off the feathers of a duck. It seemed so, on the surface, anyway. It wasn't until I started to finally mature during middle age that something inside me started seeking the more that was "out there". By "out there" I mean that there *had* to be something more than all the craziness the world had to offer. The really interesting thing about me seeking the something out there is that it led me to realize what I was really seeking was in me!

It started with me gravitating and devouring any and all books and teachings I could find that dealt with anything that had to do with inspiration, motivation, and positivity. I started at ground zero of positivity with the foundation block of positive thinking, Dr. Norman Vincent Peale's, *The Power of Positive Thinking*. This book was the very first time I had ever even heard of such a thing – that my positive thoughts had the power, combined with faith in a Creator – to create positive things and results in my life. What a concept! Now, with this light bulb that had turned on above my head, I started reading every book even closely related to it – *Think & Grow Rich*, by Napoleon Hill, *Awaken the Giant Within* by Anthony Robbins, *Manifest Your Destiny* by Dr. Wayne Dyer, *The Spontaneous Fulfillment of Your Desire* by Dr. Deepak Chopra, etc. Now this positive thinking, inspired mind started to open up to what was already in me, and evidently had always been in me just waiting for me to find it and use it.

Perhaps the biggest influence on me during this phase in my life was the book *Tough Times Never Last but Tough People Do* by Dr. Robert H. Schuller. For decades Schuller had a TV ministry called *The Hour of Power* that was broadcast weekly around the world. Even though I grew up completely agnostic, his profound passionate preaching and teaching a combination of positive thinking, motivation, and inspiration, and having faith in something greater than myself, greater than the world, propelled me to the next level of consciousness that *anything* is possible. As a matter of fact, I grabbed a hold of this concept and ran with it – literally!

Being a runner who ran on a daily basis, and now feeling empowered with my own positive thinking and belief in myself, I came up with the seemingly impossible idea that I could run 52 marathons in 52 weeks to help make the world a better place. That's running a 26.2-mile race once a week for a year! Despite having only run nine marathons in my entire life up until that time, I really believed that I could, and having met a young five-year old boy, Glen Miller, Jr. of Logan, Ohio, who had leukemia, I decided to use my 52 marathons to raise money and awareness to help find a cure for little Glen and all other victims of this disease. So, on May 5, 1996, I left behind my job of 16 years, rented out my beautiful home that I had owned in the wooded beauty of Hocking County, Ohio, and went off on my year-long adventure of running and raising money and awareness for leukemia. And boy, did I ever find out that tough times never last but tough people do!

It wasn't until years later when I started to connect with the concepts of just what the Law of Attraction is – *like attracts like,* and *that which you think and dwell upon is attracted into your life* – I realized that I was a practitioner of this powerful law without even realizing it. I came to understand that all of my successes and defeats during my year of marathoning came about by my attracting via my intense thoughts and focus. I attracted it *all* to myself, both good and bad.

An example of my attracting the good things during my year of running marathons came during the running of my fourth marathon, the Coeur d' Alene Marathon in Idaho on my birthday, May 26, 1996. I had started the year without having any idea how all of the money I needed to accomplish 52 marathons in 52 weeks. However, I was continuously radiating powerful, energized thoughts and emotions of "Hey world! I need some help here! Anything you can send me will be a big help!" Without even knowing what the Law of Attraction was, it responded accordingly in sending me most everything I needed to successfully keep running. When I made it to Coeur d' Alene, a wonderful young woman named Gayle Jacklin, who was not only the marathon race director, but the defending champion, put me up for three days for free at her beautiful home at no cost. Come race day, I had a great 26.2 mile run, but Gayle once again was the overall female champion. Since it also happened to be my birthday, while Gayle went to her champion's trophy, she asked me to drive her sports car home, as her boyfriend would drive her back. Once Gayle and I had both recovered and refreshed after the race, Gayle then proceeded to make me a birthday dinner complete with a cake! Plus, her six-year-old daughter sang happy birthday to me! I had literally attracted a home-like, happy atmosphere on my special day filled with joy and abundance. When I drove out of the town the next day, I did so with a cooler full of sandwiches that Gayle had made for me to take on the road. As I drove the many hours to my next race, I felt like I was glowing with gratitude that I had attracted into my life and experience.

What made me understand that I was practicing the Law of Attraction, and that it even existed, was the natural evolution of my seeking out reading and teachings that could help me to find the unlimited and untapped power that already was within me. Books like *Ask & It Is Given* by Esther and Jerry Hicks, and of course, *The Secret* by Rhonda Byrne finally solidified the knowing that the Law of Attraction really does exist, it really does work 24 hours a day, 7 days a week, and is never, ever turned off. It was then synchronicity grabbed a hold of me, and I found out that I could learn to become a Law of Attraction life coach via an organization led by a lady named Christy Whitman from Montreal, Canada, called the Quantum Success Coaching Academy.

As I studied and now consciously practiced the Law of Attraction, I, like so many others, struggled with trying to consistently use it to manifest the things and the life I wanted to be, do, and have in my life. I was able to manifest some things, but other times I seemed to fall flat on my face with it. Once again, I turned to explore what was within me that I could use and do to become a consistent co-creator with the Law of Attraction. In doing so, I found more books and teachings to help me accomplish just that. *The* book that finally cemented the understanding I needed to become that consistent manifester of all the good, lovely, joyful, happy, peaceful, abundant, and healthy things I desired is *A Course in Miracles.*

Once you start your study of The Course, it will become apparent to you that it is a beautiful spiritual bridge to your understanding of how to become a joyful, and consistent co-creator with the Universe via the Law of Attraction. You come to realize that in order for this to happen your life *has* to be based on the eternal Universal spiritual truths of All-That-Is, which is not of this ego-driven, illusion-filled world. The essential teaching of the all-encompassing Love in this spiritual doctrine called *A Course in Miracles* is the glue that brings it all together.

A Beautiful Symbiotic Relationship

By now you should be realizing the very real power the Law of Attraction, and that by aligning with it you can create the life you truly desire. This happens through using the energy of your own thoughts, focus and consistent persistence. When doing this you must be in complete, resonant, energetic alignment with that which you so greatly desire in order to manifest into your physical reality. Now that you understand that the Law of Attraction is completely objective, you know you must be consistently persistent in your focus on the good, joyful, abundant, healthy things you want so that they will be delivered to you. Unfortunately, the majority of the people in the world project thoughts and emotions (real energy) that fluctuate wildly between good and bad, love and hate, judgment and love, hope and worry, etc. Rare is it the person who can consistently manifest only the good, wanted things into their life. With this observation in mind, thus the main purpose of this book comes into clear focus.

As I have learned more and more about the Law of Attraction, and attempted to be a more conscious co-creator with the Universe, and because I was only sporadically consistent with my manifestations of that which I desired, I really started to wonder how I could truly consistently manifest all of the good things I wanted. It was frustrating to know that I could fairly consistently manifest a good parking spot at the shopping center, but not the $10,000 I so wanted in my bank account. I finally looked at the happenings of our daily world and realized because of the ego-driven consciousness and perception of the majority of the world and realized that we all stand on a shaky personal foundation – one that could collapse at any moment. Integrity does not seem to be a standard or even a recognizable term to most people. The best examples of this are the people who sit at the highest level of worldwide visibility – the movie stars, politicians, and sports icons. They seem to have it all – looks, talent, money, love, power, but then one after the other come crashing down into the dust, because their personal integrity lacked a rock-solid foundation based on non-dualistic Universal Truths. Without these key building blocks of Universal Truths and Integrity, their entire being, their life, rested on a shaky personal foundation that did not take much jostling to cause it to come tumbling down.

The scary thing about this observation is that the process of people's lives, their personal foundation, crashing down into debris and dust, has been going on year after year, decade after decade, century after century, millennia after millennia! In other words, it's been going for the entire history of mankind! So where does it stop? Or does it?

Make a Choice

The answer is that it can stop quickly if you make a choice – a choice for the right-minded, non-dualistic spiritual and Universal truths I have been mentioning.

This is your choice to make, no one else, only you can make it. In doing so, you will end this vicious cycle that has and continues to plague mankind for all of time. In doing so you release yourself from thoughts of separation from everything you think is outside of yourself – your brothers and sisters on planet earth, and your deep-seated belief that you are not part of All-That-Is. You release yourself from judgment. You release yourself from beliefs in guilt and sin. You release yourself from anger and attack. And in doing so, your "house", your life – the entire foundation of your being grows stronger and invulnerable, because you have made the choice for right-mindedness and

Love. When you choose this path everything thing is rectified, healed, and made whole, and a foundation based in these principles will stand for the ages.

The only reason anyone would ever *not* make this choice is because in doing so they believe that they are giving up something they think is valuable. I ask, are pain, chaos, attack, judgment, hate, guilt, and sin something you consider valuable? Incredible as it may sound, based in the thinking and beliefs of this ego-driven, dualistic world, the answer is yes. But do not give up hope that making the correct right-minded choice in your life is possible, because the chaotic, insane, decaying, dying world that you see is only an illusion – it is not real! These egotistic lessons that "that's just the way the world is and always will be" have been pounded relentlessly into our head since the moment we were born that we've come to believe that that is real. Nothing could be farther from the truth because this ego-driven living and learning is simply a smokescreen that seems like a brick wall that keeps you from seeing the simple truth of All-That-Is Oneness and uncompromising Love and Truth is your only real, true self.

"The lessons you have taught yourself have been so overlearned and fixed they rise like heavy curtains to obscure the simple and the obvious."

A Course in Miracles, T-31.1.3:3-4

Chapter 8:

THE 3 PILLARS OF YOUR FOUNDATION: Pillar #1 - MENTAL

With these thoughts of helping you to make the choice for right-mindedness to make the personal foundation of your life stand strong, I turn now to the 3 pillars of your being – Mental, Physical, and Spiritual.

When I first came up with the idea that these 3 pillars are the key to becoming a powerful, consistent manifester of the life you truly desire, I well understood already that this life is simply an illusion of our dream that we – each of us – are separate from God. Because of the deep-seated, unconscious guilt that we have from believing that we had done God wrong by believing we are now no longer one with Him, we believe He is out for vengeance and wants to kill us. This is the cause of this cycle of decay, cruelty, violence, and dying that we imagine is "reality" here in this life. And then I had a bit of an epiphany...

If we are seemingly stuck here in the illusion of this life (lifetimes), why not take positive steps to make the journey here in this illusion as a body, as best, and enjoyable as possible? That's when the idea of The 3 Pillars came to me. Your mental process and beliefs, your physical body, and your spiritual thoughts and understanding must be the key to creating a joyful, happy, loving, healthy, and abundant life – even if it really is an illusion!

"Sit down before fact like a little child, and be prepared to give up every preconceived notion, follow humbly wherever and to what abyss Nature leads you, or you shall learn nothing."
- T.H. Huxley

After struggling for many, many years trying to find the right formula to create the positive self-change in myself, and the life I desired to live that I so *desperately* sought – but was continually frustrated in achieving, I finally cracked the code and gained a clarity of understanding! That epiphany of clarity was that it takes a solid personal foundation before your desired change and manifestations can be achieved! What I share with you within these pages will help you to achieve the results, the desires, the joys, the abundance, the happiness your goals – *now* – without having to travel the long, frustrating journey that I did.

By the time you finish reading this you will understand how to:
- Utilize and integrate these 3 simple, but key pillars, into your life to create a permanent, solid foundation upon which you can build your dream "house", your life!
- Proceed to build your "house", your desired life upon this now rock-solid foundation using these solid, proven universal principles!

Ok, so you've got these ultimate dreams, goals, and desires that you have laid out in your Master Dream list – at least in your mind, and maybe even in an outline along with a few affirmations. That's a good start, however, as I suggested earlier, for these things to manifest into your life, you need to build a solid personal foundation as a person, before you can proceed with seeing them come into your reality. The 3 Pillars that I offer here will be the key to seeing your dreams manifest for you as fully as possible. Remember the purpose of a pillar – to supply the key support element for an entire structure. The full weight of the structure rests squarely on this pillar. One crack or weakness in one single pillar can lead to the collapse of the entire structure, or at the least the entire structure being very shaky! You may have two out of three of your pillars rock-solid, but if one of them has a weakness, then that entire structure – your dreams, goals, and desires, are not resting on a reliable foundation. To achieve that which you truly desire, your first job is to make sure your personal foundation is rock-solid by strengthening your pillars! With this is mind, let's look at the first pillar.

This first pillar is your mental wellbeing – your overall outlook on the world, the people around you, and, of course, yourself. Your mental pillar categorically represents all your desires, goals, wants, and ultimate dreams. Unfortunately, the world has come to assume that negativity is the normal way of viewing reality, however, this "normal" view of reality leads to a constant drain on the energy of your daily life, health, and well-being – it's not productive, but destructive! To create this solid Mental pillar within yourself, first you must change how you view the world, and yourself. It is time for you to do a 180-degree turn-around and establish in your mind the capacity to finally let go of all thoughts and paradigms of lack, attack, and judgment. Now is the time to let go of all addictions and self-medication. It is time for you to turn on the "light" within your mind and create a rock- solid mental pillar of the things that will produce more energy, enthusiasm, non- judgment, optimistic, self-love, productive and abundant thoughts, intense desire, plus very real trust, and faith! This *new* mental pillar of yours will then allow you to work as a co-creator with the Universe, as everything that is needed to bring about your dreams and desires and is then unfolded and orchestrated to reach fulfillment. This new mental pillar that you have achieved works hand-in-hand with the very definition and workings of the Law of Attraction – "Like attracts like!" Without the drain and strain of your old shaky, negative mental pillar, you will start to see very real, positive progress manifesting in your life as you are now resonating, vibrating, and marching in step with that which you wish to create in your life. If you take to heart what I suggest here for your mental pillar, it literally will be as if you had taken some fresh concrete, and patched up that energy-draining, non- productive, negative, big 'ol crack that you previously had in your mental pillar! So now, Pillar #1, your Mental Pillar, is rock solid, and now has the capability of keeping your "house," the entire structure of your dreams, goals, and desires, upright and solid with confidence it will not collapse.

We're Pre-Programmed

It's no wonder that we all must deal with issues with our mental capacities and perceptions, and then find it hard in finding balance within the realm of right-minded thinking.

Bruce Lipton's book, *Spontaneous Evolution*, clarifies just why we all must overcome from the get-go of our lives, an unbalanced mental pillar. Referring to brainwave studies done on children using an electroencephlogram (EEG), "*The predominant delta and theta* {brain waves} *activity expressed by children younger than six signifies that their brains are operating at levels below consciousness. Delta and theta brain frequencies define a brain state known as a hypnogogic trance – the same neural state that hypnotherapists use to directly download new behaviors into the subconscious minds of their clients. In other words, the first six years of a child's life are spent in a hypnotic trance! A child's perceptions of the world are directly downloaded into the subconscious during this time, without discrimination and without filters of the analytical self-conscious mind, which doesn't fully exist. Consequently, our fundamental perceptions about life and our role in it are learned without our having the capacity to choose or reject those beliefs. We are simply programmed.*"

This gives us a clear picture of why there is mental confusion within the mental pillar of virtually every single human on the planet! By the time we are six years old, we've been pre-programmed by our families and everyone around us with all their judgments, misinformation, unloving paradigms, and then carry it with us the rest of our lives. There are those few people who are able to overcome this hypnotic-type programming during childhood to walk and live in true right-mindedness, but unfortunately the vast majority of the people of this world *never* overcome their misguided childhood perceptual programming. It's no wonder many spiritual and scientific thinkers and teachers consider the world to be insane! One view of the daily newscast or read of your local newspaper would seem to verify this!

This is why this book has been written for you – to open your minds, your eyes, and your heart to finally realize, "*Wait? You mean I started this life out in a mental deficit of pre-programmed wrong thinking and perception?*" And upon this startling epiphany, you can start that mental pivot toward a right-minded thought process.

The Benefits of Creating a Solid Mental Pillar

So right now, imagine yourself with a now-healed mind – one whose thoughts and choices truly blossom from a place of spiritual integrity and eternal Universal Truths. Finding yourself in this state should allow you to enjoy the benefits of doing so. You'll realize that you can now move forward with your life in complete confidence. This confidence emerges from the deep knowing trust and faith that comes with aligning your mind with Source, All-That-Is – God. It's realizing that you are completely and totally cared for in every manner, and the result is an unerring confidence in all that you do.

Eliminating any and all cracks in your mental pillar is the first step toward learning how to consistently work hand-in-hand with the Law of Attraction. This new right-mindedness of yours creates consistency in your daily life, your thoughts, and your life force. With this new right-minded mentality, you walk in complete harmony with your Source.

This quote from David Hoffmeister's book, *This Moment Is Your Miracle*, makes it very clear just how powerful doing so becomes.

"Rather than living in fear of the possible reactions of others, we become authentic and stay in integrity with the truth. We extend the love and the happiness. We are empowered by love. From the clarity, the direction can only be integrity of mind, where everything we desire is in alignment with God, with our right-mindedness."

The key words in David's quote, "*authentic, integrity, truth, love, happiness, empowered, clarity, alignment*, and *right-mindedness*", resonate perfectly with the idea of healing and making whole the mental pillar of your being. This is the correct path for you to walk as you seek to fortify all three of your pillars and establish that rock-solid personal foundation that will stand for the ages. Especially his statement, "*...where everything we desire is in alignment with God in our right-mindedness*", is totally indicative of how healing and strengthening your mental pillar can and will put you in perfect alignment with the Law of Attraction (remember, the L.O.A. is really love!) to consistently co-create with the Universe all the good that you desire to be in your life.

Your strategy for building a solid Mental Pillar lies in following the path of right-minded living and thinking is doable. You just need to make the choice to do so, and then put it in practice. You, making the conscious decision to follow the path of spiritual right-minded integrity, in addition to repeating positive affirmations with dogged determination, is a powerful formula to your success.

Suggested Affirmations:

One excellent strategy for building or re-building your mental pillar is done via the repetition of affirmations. Constantly repeating your affirmations, especially when stated with strong emotion, will continually increase the attraction energy necessary for them to manifest into your physical reality.

- *My thoughts are now working in harmony and resonance with the Universe in helping me to manifest all my greatest dreams, goals, and desires!*

- *I am now moving forward with deep trust and faith in creating that which I desire for my life knowing that my mind and thoughts now rest on a rock-solid foundation!*

- *My thoughts and visualizations of my ultimate dreams, goals, and desires manifesting in my life now flow easily and effortlessly, because my mental pillar is now based on solid, healthy, productive Universal principles!*

- *I now know that I am building my "house" on a rock-solid foundation based on the strength, truth, and love of my new mental pillar!*

Chapter 9

THE 3 PILLARS OF YOUR FOUNDATION: #2 - PHYSICAL

Our first pillar, *Mental*, may seem somewhat abstract, simply because it is not something solid that you can see or touch. Even though your mental pillar is composed of real energy, you, of course, cannot see it physically, and seems to therefore be an abstract concept. Our second pillar, *Physical*, is also composed of real energy, but it is a concrete concept/entity, because you can see, feel, and perceive your body. This pillar can represent weight loss goals, sports goals, health & wellbeing, and nutrition. When it comes to making sure that your physical pillar is sound and sturdy enough to support your entire "house", anyone who has ever had an injury or illness knows that her "house" is on shaky ground, at least for a while until it heals. Your physical pillar is every bit as important as your mental pillar, in that it equally shares the load of the entire structure of your being. Our world's population continues to exist on a shaky physical foundation as more and more new diseases and maladies continue to attack the body. Preventable problems such as obesity and diabetes go hand-in-hand with high blood pressure, and many other chronic health issues. Stunningly poor nutrition through lack of knowledge or stubbornness, also contribute to undermining your physical being, and creating that big symbolic, but real "crack" in this all-important pillar. The incredible thing is that all of these physical problems come on the heels of ever-increasing knowledge and understanding of health care, medicine, nutrition, and exercise. Vast portions of the world's populace *are* doing the right things to their bodies to make their physical pillar sound, strong, and healthy – yet even more of the world's population neglects this key pillar of their body, and allows it to crumble, and undermine their entire being. If your physical self is not in working order, then those other two important pillars will not hold up the entire "house" on their own – at least not for long anyway.

Let me be clear that I am not talking about if you have a major health impairment or genetic disability. I am speaking about doing the necessary, doable health, fitness, and hygiene maintenance routines that help keep your Physical Pillar in excellent condition. And even if you do suffer from any type of major health issue or physical disability, these daily physical maintenance rituals can only be beneficial, and hopefully increase the quality of your life.

The How To's:

Many of the ideas for creating and maintaining a strong, healthy physical pillar that I propose here, are not new, however, they are worthy of review, contemplation, and implementation. Here are some key "How To's" that you can use to build your physical pillar –

- Regular, consistent exercise is the first place you need to start. While you may have reacted to this statement with "Duh!", please understand that while exercise is almost universally accepted as one of the best ways to build a strong body, it is also one of the first to be rejected because it may be seen as too much effort and too hard.

- Intelligent, balanced nutrition and diet are right up there as key items in producing your sound physical pillar. This is another topic that is generally acknowledged worldwide as important to a healthy body but is either ignored or poo-poo'ed by many.

- Good health care, and personal hygiene also are key components in creating and maintaining sound physical structure no matter what your culture, socio-economic status, religion, or race.

Let's take a closer look at these solid physical pillar attributes: Many people shun exercise simply because it is too hard. The intense effort that is necessary to drop excessive body weight, produce muscle, and balance out your aerobic and cardiovascular system does take a lot of sweat-inducing effort, but oh, the results! To the person who says to me that exercise is "too much work and effort!" I say, "OK, just think of how much time and effort it took to get your body *out* of shape, and 50 pounds overweight!" Without exception, the work, effort, and sweat that it does take to "right the ship" of your body via exercise, has merit to no end! Create and maintain a body that has low body fat, proper body weight, toned and strong muscles, low blood pressure and cholesterol, and a lower stress level, and I say your "house" is going to stand on solid ground that will endure for a long time. As for the nutritional aspect needed to maintain your physical pillar, there can be some stunningly stubborn attitudes and ideas about it, despite an inherent knowing that you *should* be eating healthy foods, and not over-indulging in excessive calories. Truly smart, healthy nutrition should be a "no brainer," but it mystifyingly remains not so. Living on a diet of high fat, overly salted or sugar saturated fast food does not a strong physical pillar make, yet masses of people do exactly that. Again, an argument could be made that mass media and commercialization perpetuate poor diets via advertising, and fad diets, but once again, this does not change the fact the correct foods in proper proportions and moderation is one of the paths to establishing and maintaining your sound physical pillar. And finally maintaining and using good health care and hygiene are also necessities that keep those deadly cracks from forming in your physical pillar.

Modern medicine – be it traditional, or holistic and alternative medicine, now stands at a pinnacle of knowledge and practice in the history of the world. The same holds true for personal hygiene in that every form of good grooming, and body maintenance is readily available to you.

The bottom line is this: Regular exercise, intelligent nutrition, and good health care and grooming create a strong, sound physical pillar for your "house" to endure and stand upright for the ages.

As earlier stated, your physical pillar does not seem so abstract as your other two pillars because you can feel it. This does not change the truth that you are a spiritual being having a human experience, and your body really *is* just a dream of assembled energy causing you to believe it is solid matter. *A Course in Miracles* teaches that your body is simply a communication device that the Holy Spirit can utilize to help you and your brothers in the world to awaken from this dream.

"The body is the means by which God's Son returns to sanity. Though it was made to fence him into hell without escape yet has the goal of Heaven been exchanged for the pursuit of hell. The Son of God extends his hand to reach his brother and to help him walk along the road with him. Now it serves to heal the mind that it was made to kill."

- From the Workbook for Students in A Course in Miracles

Reading this quote is meant to emphasize that if you only perceive your body from the ego's view, your physical pillar will never become strong for the ages. And even though you may achieve enlightenment and awakening within your current lifetime and body, it will still eventually die. However, if you strengthen your physical pillar, you will be able to enjoy a body that stays strong, healthy, and productive right until the end because you chose to live in right-mindedness and alignment with the eternal universal truth of oneness and love.

Now let us be clear as to why having an unhealthy physical pillar can block the Law of Attraction from working symbiotically to create the good things you desire in your life. Anytime your physical pillar is out of accord with good health and fitness it is because your mind is still thinking and projecting from the ego-driven thought system. The ego's thought system is one based on chaos, inconsistency, attack, lack, and guilt. *Any* thought system based on these principles (which is *all* the ego can ever know) can only be based in a low energy vibrating realm that will only attract more of the same. Consequently, you continue to attract more unhealthy, destructive energy to your body. The ego's thought system is actually insane and results in perpetual wrong-minded, upside-down thinking. The way to heal your physical pillar is to do as is suggested here and pivot your thinking 180 degrees to that of right-minded thinking and integrity based on eternal spiritual truth. Doing so will immediately start to raise the vibrational energy level of your mind and body, and align you with attracting all of the good, happy, loving and abundant things you desire to be in your life.

The combination of common-sense physical care and your understanding of what your body really is, is a beautiful synthesis of "crystalized light", truly will strengthen your physical pillar.

Suggested Affirmations:

• *I am now seeing the healthy benefits and results in my body of my doing regular exercises every day.*

- *I quickly noticed an increase in my clarity, a healthy weight loss, and more energy and zip in my step now that I am eating healthier and making smart choices with my diet.*

- *I now feel better, more confident, and lively since I started taking pride in my grooming, clothing, and cleanliness.*

- *I now practice a happy balance of common-sense physical care and the understanding that my body is neutral, and a communication device with the Holy Spirit, to live a long, happy, and healthy life right to its end.*

Chapter 10:

THE 3 PILLARS OF YOUR FOUNDATION #3 - SPIRITUAL

Now we come to the third of the three pillars that provide the foundation of your being so that you can live the life you truly desire – built on sound, eternal principles. Pillar number three is Spiritual. While I give equal credence to all three pillars, I will say that if one of those three may carry a heavier load in holding up your house, it is this one. The best way I can summarize your Spiritual pillar is that it is living, thinking, and acting with right-mindedness that is based on the eternal Universal truths and laws. It is living and acting with integrity in all that you say, do, and think. It is walking the walk and talking the talk in alignment and resonance with your true, Divine inner Self. In a world that is based on paradigms of lack and attack, judgment, guilt, and feelings of unworthiness, this Spiritual pillar may be the hardest of the three to fortify and keep standing solidly without wavering. Now let's look at why the Spiritual pillar can be challenging.

Throughout history spiritual doctrines such as Buddhism, the Hindu Vedanta, and now *A Course in Miracles*, have categorically stated that this life, this world is but a dream, an illusion of the ego. In this dream, we think we are separate from our Creator, which causes us to live in a dualistic reality. This dualistic perspective leads to this idea of separation – from religions, in language, in races, and causes an infinite number of perspectives about every possible subject in the world. Unfortunately, based in this dualistic realm, our perception is based on the deception of the dream of separation.

I noted earlier the phrase that "truth is union", and that is what you should strive for in seeking to make your spiritual pillar rock solid so that your house may stand forever. In this union, this oneness, lies all the eternal Universal truths and laws, and are not, nor ever will be, subject to the changing whims, perspectives, and judgments of this world. *This* is where your spiritual pillar solidifies and stands strong – forever! When you base your life on this union and oneness with the eternal Universal, Divine truths, *then* there is no fear that your house will come crashing down because of a poor foundation. If you continue to base your spiritual pillar on the ever-shifting sands of the world's perspectives of lack and attack, you will *never* achieve the solid foundations based on the strength of your three personal pillars, and the likelihood of your house to come crashing down grows exponentially.

The How To's:

- Trust in the wisdom of the eternal Universal truths of Love, Light, and Oneness with your Creator – the "All-That-Is."

- Let go of the dream of being separate from your brothers around the world, whatever their religion, creed, or color.

- Let go of the idea of being separate from the Creator.

- Practice non-judgment, defenselessness, and forgiveness in every moment, and in every situation.

- Don't just practice this in your mind, but in your daily life. Put your new, solid spiritual pillar into action!

If upon reading these "How To's" you may be asking yourself, "How can I implement these? They are so radical from what I have been taught my whole life!" I understand this, but I assure you that as you commit yourself to studying and practicing right-minded spiritual thinking and integrity, these "How To's" will become more and more clear. As the light of understanding the universal unity and oneness of All-That-Is dawns upon your mind, what was once unfathomable now flows easily and effortlessly to help shift your mind into alignment with a higher vibrational energy of attracting all good and loving things to you. You must have a powerful desire to finally let go of the ego's thought system to successfully practice and live these spiritual "How To's".

Suggested Affirmations:

- *I have now let go of all beliefs, judgments, and ideas of lack and attack.*

- *I now practice daily forgiving and loving all people, animals, and anything else that I once believed were separate from me.*

- *I walk the walk of living my life based on all the eternal, unchanging Universal Truths.* (As discussed in the chapter "The Seven Essential Universal Laws")

- *I now understand that truth is union, and darkness and ignorance disappear in its light.*

As with the suggested "How To's", the same practice of letting go of the ego's destructive, unproductive thought system applies. As always, persistent repetition of these powerful affirmations will shift your energy into alignment with the Law of Attraction to manifest them into your life.

Bonus!
The Keystone: Forgiveness

This bonus pillar, Forgiveness, is perhaps, a surprise to you. You may be asking yourself right now, "How the heck does forgiveness have anything to do with creating a strong foundation for me?" Think of forgiveness as the cement that holds your 3 pillars in place and has filled in and smoothed over the cracks that had existed. However, the best way to think of forgiveness is that it is the keystone you set in place to keep the structure upright. Spiritual teachers, psychologists and psychotherapists have noted that many personal and sometimes chronic issues – mental, physical, and spiritual issues - disappear when you forgive long held grudges, hatred, judgments, or resentments. Without forgiveness, these issues can fester both consciously and unconsciously and can many times manifest themselves in the form of health problems. Without forgiveness, long held negative beliefs and thoughts sap the very wellbeing and energy right out of you and are insidious because you may not understand that living your life without forgiving is *the* source of many of your problems. However, the type of forgiveness that I speak of now is not the same forgiveness as the world practices now. The forgiveness I refer to is of perfect spiritual forgiveness, or as many spiritual teachers call it, *Quantum Forgiveness*.

Why do I call it "Quantum Forgiveness"? Because it is a type of forgiveness unlike the ego's thought system-based type of forgiveness as the world practices it. First let me clear up any misperception of how the word "quantum" is used in regard to the type of forgiveness I am talking about. The dictionary's definition of the world quantum means "the smallest amount of physical quantity that can exist independently." Many of you may know the word from the study of the field of Quantum Physics. Yes, quantum does mean digging down to that infinitely small quantity, which in the case of the field of physics involves studying subatomic levels of physical realities such as protons, neutrinos, electrons, etc. People have pointed out to me that using the word quantum in conjunction with the word forgiveness makes no sense in that they think I am discussing the tiniest quantity of forgiveness. Let me make a distinction here that will clarify matching these two words together.

What happens when you take that quantum leap down to the sub atomic level and you think you can go no further in your search for any more that exists, suddenly a wormhole (as astrophysicists refer to) opens up and you cross over into and open up to another gargantuan, infinite universe of existence, different dimensions, and unlimited possibilities that you never even knew existed! Your journey into the quantum realm actually changes the definition from the smallest of the small to All-That-Is – infinite possibilities and existence! It's a phenomenon of experiencing infinity. Any Quantum physicist who has done research in this field will verify this for you. Thus, with this understanding, quantum transcends from the smallest of the small to the greatest of the great – infinity, All-That-Is. Knowing this makes it easy to understand why the word "quantum" works seamlessly and perfectly with the word "forgiveness"! Quantum & Forgiveness are in perfect resonance and alignment with each other.

The way the world has and still does practice what it calls "forgiveness" is that when you forgive someone or something that you think has wronged you, you do so from a perspective of being on a higher, more self-righteous level. You're up "here," and the "sinner" you are forgiving is "down there." You say you "forgive" them, but in truth you feel that this forgiveness you give them is an unwarranted gift that must uphold their guilt you would "forgive." As *A Course in Miracles* states,

---

> *"Unjustified forgiveness is attack. And this is all the world can ever give. It pardons 'sinners' sometimes but remains aware that they have sinned. And so it does not merit the forgiveness that it gives."*

Quantum Forgiveness or true spiritual forgiveness is based on what I said earlier that this life is but a dream of separation from the Creator where all is one. This world is a dualistic dream of unfairness, cruelty, judgment, and attack. In other words, it is *not real*! Looking for clarity on this topic leads us back to more from the A.C.I.M.

"Pardon is always justified. It has a sure foundation. (author's note: note the word "foundation" in relation to the 3 Pillars!) You do not forgive the unforgivable, nor overlook a real attack that calls for punishment. If pardon were unjustified, you would be asked to sacrifice your rights when you return forgiveness for attack. But you merely asked to see forgiveness as the natural reaction to distress that rests on error, and thus calls for help. Forgiveness is the only sane response. It keeps your rights from being sacrificed."

Practicing true Quantum Forgiveness is based in the Universal Truth of Love and acknowledges the fact that nothing has really happened to forgive because it is not real – it is but a dream of this world. Quantum Forgiveness is an understanding that all is One, and you stand in Oneness with your brother, with your Creator. As author, Gary Renard states in his book, *Love Has Forgotten No One*, *"...forgiveness is the home of miracles, because the miracle is forgiveness."*

The final piece of the puzzle to building your strong personal foundation based on the 3 Pillars of mental, physical, and spiritual, is forgiveness. Think of true Quantum Forgiveness as the keystone you set in place that is the final piece that holds your "house" together and keeps it from collapsing.

The How To's:

- When you feel that you have been wronged or attacked in anyway, immediately say to yourself, "*You are forgiven. All is let go and released.*"

- Acknowledge to yourself that any wrong aimed your way is an illusion of the ego, and there really is nothing to forgive. Forgive it anyway.

- Take a moment to recognize forgiveness as being merited, and it will heal any wrong.

SUGGESTED AFFIRMATIONS:

- *I know that forgiveness is a miracle, and I now let miracles replace all grievances*

- *I am grateful that I now understand that forgiveness is my function as the light of the world.*

- *I am now practicing true Quantum forgiveness that does not use fear to undo fear and allows me to simply overlook error that is not real.*

- *When I practice true forgiveness, I am forgiving illusions, and not the truth.*

Once you understand that making all three elements of your being - mental, physical, and spiritual – your "pillars" – as strong as possible...and with the keystone of forgiveness as the final rock set in place as the key to your "house" standing strong for the ages, then you will appreciate this very powerful quote from Abraham-Hicks:

"There is nothing that you cannot be, do, or have!"

So, I offer you this simple little formula to live your life by – a formula with great power to help you create and live the life you desire, based on the eternal, Universal Truths.

TL + LH + F = TLP
(Tread Lightly + Love Heartily + Forgiveness = True Love & Peace)

Chapter 11

Why Creating a Rock-Solid Personal Foundation Is Crucial

"Therefore, everyone who hears these words of mine and puts them into practice is like a wise man who built his house on the rock. The rain came down, the streams rose, and the winds blew and beat against that house; yet it did not fall, because it had its foundation on the rock. But everyone who hears these words of mine and does not put them into practice is like a foolish man who built his house on sand. The rain came down, the streams rose, and the winds blew and beat against that house, and it fell with a great crash."

Matthew 7:24 – 27 (NIV)

So far in this book I have laid out all the elements necessary to cohesively build your life - *the 3 Pillars of your mental, physical, and spiritual being, a foundation for your life that is your unmovable base, and the keystone of your life, Quantum Forgiveness.*

When this doesn't happen then it becomes like the old children's nursery rhyme of Humpty Dumpty.

Humpty Dumpty sat on a wall,
Humpty Dumpty had a great fall.
All the king's horses and all the king's men
Couldn't put Humpty together again.

If you remember, Humpty was an egg with human-like characteristics, and when he fell off the wall his eggshell shattered into thousands of pieces, that nobody was able to put back together. In other words, Humpty Dumpty's great fall is just like that which I have been describing in which the huge cracks in the pillars of an individual cause their entire life to come crashing down – and when this happens it is difficult to put that life back together again. If that person's life is resurrected in some manner, it most likely will never even closely resemble that which it could have been had they erected a rock-solid personal foundation for their life, supported by three strong-for-the-ages pillars.

I truly doubt if there is a single person reading this right now that does *not* want their life to stand up strong to weather the storms and forces of life. Perhaps only those with suicidal tendencies may consider it, but by then they have completely acquiesced to the ego's grand illusion of total and complete separateness from Source. I imagine that a person like this, lives only in a black tunnel of despair where there is no possibility of light or illumination to snap them out of this spiral to death. However, bleak this may sound, I know that this is not you, because you are here right now, right here with me on our search for hope, light, and truth! The good news is we've found all three of these, and it really is possible to live your entire life with these beautiful benefits of walking, living, and resonating in the integrity of the Universal truth of Oneness and unconditional love.

As for the question of why it is now, more than ever, crucial to create a base and a personal support system that will endure forever? It's not like the people of the world are not trying to do so, but because they are still stuck in the dimension of the ego's dualistic thought-system, they either don't know where to look to find this "something better " life, or they always look in the wrong places – especially where there is no light or hope (although at times they *think* they see a glimmer of light).

All you need do is turn on your television to the news, open the newspaper, or tune in to talk radio, and you will see, read, and hear that there are millions of people demonstrating, rioting, and striving with their lives to find that something better that they so ardently desire – and yet all they find is there doesn't seem to be *any* light at the end of the tunnel. They may achieve some positive resolutions to their conflict, but it almost never lasts. This is because all conflict is based in our ego-based thought system. And when they do finally achieve the result, they so ardently desired, by then it will be so convoluted and distorted, they will continue their unending journey in disgust and unfulfillment, seeking that "something better" in yet another desired result. It is ever the ego's pronouncement of, "*Seek and do not find*" and that will always be their result as they continue to walk the un-awakened path. If you examine the non-stop drama, unending conflict, and continual war-making throughout all of human history, the only possible conclusion that you could ever come to is that the world really is insane.

To that point, author Bruce Lipton states,

"In a collective culture, judgments and reasoning are predicated on the perceived truths of the basal paradigm. Consequently, if the paradigmatic beliefs of a culture are untrue or flawed, then the population that knowingly operated under those faulty beliefs would collectively express unsound judgments and reasoning. In such a case, an entire population can be technically judged to be insane."

And those millions of people who want that something better and work and strive so hard to attain it *always* run into a stone wall. That stone wall just happens to be the millions of people who are working just as hard or harder than them to keep the world insane in their efforts to keep and maintain power, control, and wealth. Such is the powerful influence of the ego over this dualistic-based dream of a world. Of course, this is true not only of today's world, but of the entirety of human history. Again, from the perspective of all of mankind's history of conflict and non-stop struggle, there really is *no* light at the end of the tunnel!

This may make it seem like there is no escape from the ongoing human insanity, but here is hope! There is light at the end of the tunnel, and that Light is *you!* The only way to find this Light that is you, and once-and-for-all leave behind this collective culture of insanity, is to use your free will to choose to no longer believe in what the dualistic, ego-driven world has to offer you. This obviously is hard to accomplish, especially if you still have the hard-wired paradigms the world has installed in you. But if you are a seeker of the light and the *real* truth you simply must take this step to awaken from the dream. In doing so lies the remedy for the awakening of the light of the Truth in the minds and hearts of those millions currently working so hard at keeping the ego-driven insane world as the norm. Your light shines on them and gradually and purposefully dissipates their darkness.

The Buddha was asked,
"Are you a God?" They asked
"No.
An Angel?
No.
A Saint?
No.
Then what are you?"
Buddha answered, "I am awake."

When Buddha pronounces that he is "awake" he means that he has finally come out of the dream that befell the Son of God in which he has dreamed of this universe of separation from God. He finally understands that what his human eyes, ears, and brain thought was real is anything but that. He has awakened to his true divinity as the child of God. Now you may well be thinking, "*I'm no Buddha!*", but remember that this thought is still within the realm of this dream of separation from All-That-Is. You are still hanging around within that collective culture of insanity.

As Osho states in his book, *Awareness*,

"...the truth is possible only when you are not dreaming. A dreaming mind cannot see the true. A dreaming mind will convert the truth also into a dream."

So hopefully by now it is obvious what the value of creating a rock-solid personal foundation is by living and walking in the integrity of the Universal eternal spiritual truths of unconditional love and oneness, is – You are awakened!

I can already see the Buddha smiling in all-knowingness as he rejoices in your awakening. Your awakening is also your brother's awakening – the awakening of all who populate the earth. Oh, and the benefits of awakening from the ego's dream of this life are beyond compare.

"There is a way of living in the world that is not here, although it seems to be. You do not change appearance, though you smile more frequently. Your forehead is serene; your eyes are quiet." – A Course in Miracles

This is confirmed in almost all of the descriptions of the many experiences by those who have had true spiritual awakening episodes. When this happens, you see through the eyes of your Source, not through your body's eyes.

"Every thought, action, decision, or feeling creates an eddy in the interlocking, inter-

balancing energy fields of life. In this interconnected universe, every improvement we make in our private world improves the world at large for everyone." – Dr. David Hawkins

In other words, you will never see this world, your life, or the lives of others, in an interlocking chain of disunity, conflict, and death. Instead, as you walk hand-in hand with your Source you see, think, and practice only unconditional love and forgiveness, and radiate the same to all who come in contact with you.

My Personal Journey Through Life

When I was a young boy, I was a typical child in that I had vast amounts of energy and enthusiasm. I drove my parents to distraction as I was always going one hundred miles per hour racing around the house and in the yard. Then like many kids, my seemingly boundless energy would flame-out, and eventually I would conk out for the night (much to my parent's delight).

I was always wide-eyed in wonderment, and as I grew older, I channeled this huge reserve of energy and wonderment into riding my bike, delivering my newspaper route, and playing baseball. At this point in my life, my greatest desire was to play professional baseball for the Cleveland Indians, as I continued zooming through life one hundred miles per hour. When I reached my teenage years, the contrasts of life – school, girls, rebelliousness, and rock 'n roll music soon started to diminish my wide-eyed wonderment, but yet I intuitively knew that the world really was my oyster. One thing I did retain at this point in my life was that I knew that there was nothing I could not be, do, or have. However, roadblocks in reaching my dreams seemed to appear out of thin air one after the other. The paradigms that had been installed in me before I was six years old started to rear their ugly heads, and my unmitigated enthusiasm and belief in who and what I was, and what I wanted to achieve, waned badly. In fact, it all became a muddle that caused me to stall-out and keep me in the gridlock of indecision on the how's, what's, and why's of where

I was headed. Thus, I was labeled, "the boy with so much potential", because everyone else could see it, except me.

Fast forward to the boy who became a young man still bearing the label of "potential", and with no successes to prove that potential that supposedly lay within me. As with many of my fellow humans, the years passed by, and my many poor decisions, and mis-directions began to pile up. I became the personification of the classic, "one step forward, and two steps back." My victories were few and far between, and while I stayed at the peak for short amounts of time, the contrasts of life continually kicked in, and I took another two steps back. It was a vicious cycle that I had no idea how to escape.

Although it is said by the mystics and spiritual teachers that time is but an illusion, seemingly in the blink of an eye, I was now a man of middle age. Despite this seemingly endless cycle of frustration and lack of successes, somehow, someway, a crack of light started to trickle through to my mind, and slowly an awakening of that "potential" that had laid dormant for all the years, started to blossom. Without even really realizing it, something within me simply could not take it anymore. I finally decided to open the door of my mind to allow the light to shine in. I found the writings and teachings of the ones who had already accessed the light and the truth that there really is something better than what the world has to offer – ever. Hill, Schuller, Dyer, Robbins, Peale, Proctor. These teachers helped the door open within my mind and allowed even more light to shine in. Finally, the limiting beliefs of my childhood that had followed me into adulthood started to dissolve as the truth dawned in my heart and mind. It was truly an enlightening time in my life, even though I never completely shed my penchant for taking one step forward and two steps back. Finally, the two steps backward were coming fewer and farther between, and legitimate progress manifested into my life.

Yet another fast forward to the later portion of my life, now officially well past middle age. The massive amounts of light, love, and truth continued to pour daily into my life causing me to realize my true purpose to be a source of help to all I come in contact with. Yet somewhere deep within my subconscious there remained many beliefs of the body, that kept my mind in chains, unable to fully release itself into the realm of pure enlightenment and truth. Sometimes now, it was one step forward and *three* steps back!

Then one day I looked back on my life and how it had transpired thus far. I figured he had done somewhat of a good job, but I realized that I had taken many a wrong turn and made needless and countless poor choices – simply because my inner ear was not tuned to what my Divine Guide had been whispering ever so quietly, consistently, and lovingly to me at every single step of my life's journey. It was then I experienced an epiphany of Divine guidance and direction.

It happened on a hot summer evening when I headed over to a local pool for a swim. No one was around as I prepared to dive in to do a few laps, that is except for a family of ducks who were also in the pool doing a few laps of their own!

As soon as I got in the pool and starting swimming, I realized I had scared the whole family of ducks out of the water, and off they went – that is, all except the smallest baby duck who remained. Evidently, he was so small he could not muster enough power to leap from the water to the concrete lip of the pool that was several inches above the water line. In the ensuing minutes of my lap swimming, I saw this little duck swimming underwater as fast as he could from one end of the pool to the other trying to escape the swimming "giant", who he was afraid of. I was amazed at this sight! I didn't even know ducks could swim underwater like that, let alone a baby duck!

This went on and on for many, many minutes. When I would surface, there was the little guy, still unable to get out of the pool, and quacking for his mom and dad, because he was afraid, alone, and scared.

When I finally got out of the water, I watched as yet another family of ducks arrived and got in for a swim. I could see the little guy was excited to see more ducks, but alas, it wasn't his family!

My heart went out to the little guy, who was really afraid and alone, and all he wanted to do was be near the other ducks, but they chased him away because he wasn't a part of their clan.

Finally, all these other ducks left the water, and once again the baby duck was alone and stuck in this pool, quacking his heart out to escape! I wanted to try to help the little guy get out, but every time I approached, the duck went the other direction. On and on this went until finally, with a mighty leap (only because he finally found a concrete step leading out of the pool) the baby duck launched himself free of his prison, and off he went quacking his young heart out in search of his family.

As I dried myself off after my swim with this baby duck, I wasn't exactly sure why, but this episode with this stuck, lost, helpless little duck left me pretty shaken. After some deep contemplation on this experience, it was given me to realize that this episode was an analogy of my own life up to this point in time. I was then suddenly enlightened to realize that this little duck swimming under water from one end of the pool to the other, over and over and over, trying to escape what he was afraid of – and seemingly lacking the strength to escape the situation was – ME!

Yes, this was exactly what I had been doing my entire life up until this point in time, until, like this baby duck, I finally just couldn't take it anymore! I just *had* to muster all the strength I could to escape this seemingly endless cycle of fleeing what I feared without any hope of escaping, and I did. I have.

I finally took that mighty leap of faith, and went off in search of my Divine Guide, calling His name as I went (Minus the quacking! Ha ha!) And the coolest part is that He answered me, and now I hear. Now I listen. Now I follow His direction! It was then I realized just how blessed I was to have taken that mighty leap of faith.

Fortunately for me, the boy who was now an older man, the limitless power of the light of my Source, stayed true and focused, and now I take inspired action on the very real guidance that my Divine Source lovingly gives to me on a moment-to-moment basis. The truth has set me free!

I have weathered my thousands of poor choices and decisions, and overcome the hard-wired, energy-sucking, darkness-producing beliefs that had directed me in the wrong direction most of my life. I consciously decided to create a rock-solid personal foundation, and strengthen the 3 Pillars of my mental, physical, and spiritual being so they stand strong for the ages. I topped it all off with the unworldly and uncompromising keystone of Quantum Forgiveness.

The result is the boy, this man – me, regained my wide-eyed wonderment, joy, and zest for life that I came into the world with, and happily came to remember my youthful joys of life that still resided within me. I remembered my life purpose that I had always intuitively known from the start.

Begin Again

As you can see from this story of my journey through my life that was marked by the pitfalls the ego helped to generate during my life, it *is* possible to begin again. By beginning again, I mean that once you have allowed the light of the truth to dawn upon your mind, your Divine Memory that you were born with but forgot about, becomes rekindled. Once this happens, then you remember your God-given ability to exercise your free will to choose to walk in the integrity of rightmindedness. No longer are you totally restricted by the dualistic contrast and tricks of the ego, as you now understand that you have a choice – in every moment.

At this point when you can feel the light start to shine again in your mind and heart, it is hard to not become impatient. You must remember, however, just like my explanation about how everything is energy, and how it takes time to shift your energy from wrongmindedness to rightmindedness. Besides, if you experienced a 180-degree shift all at once, it might be too traumatic for you to handle. This method of awakening takes more time, but the reward will be your return to your rightful place in Heaven – in the right way, at the right time, and in a way that is done lovingly, gently, and beautifully.

Even knowing this it is hard not to be impatient, especially if you realize that it may or may not even happen within this lifetime of yours. Afterall, it is a journey in returning to your rightful home. However, don't let your frustration at learning that your full return to complete wakefulness at home in Heaven may not be completed during this lifetime. The beautiful part about this method of your gentle awakening by your Father is that you start to remember, you start to see, you start to hear, and you start to live in the light of the truth and walk in the integrity of rightmindedness. Not only are you making progress in reawakening, but because you are, so too are all your brothers throughout the world beginning their reawakening. This is because, since all is one and there really is no separation (except in the ego's mind), it is impossible that the light dawn upon your mind without you sharing it with every single other person in the world. This may seem ludicrous to the mind still locked within an ego driven thought system, but it is the truth.

Summary – Scientists have finally caught up with what the spiritual teachers have been saying throughout all of history. This lends credence that we are all connected. Consequently, *all* of your thoughts and actions affect every single other person in humankind, without exception! And although this understanding may not have reached your mind yet, once you finally allow the light of the truth, of All-That-Is, start to shine upon your being, you then come to intuitively understand what the scientists are now concluding.

You don't have to be a quantum physicist to understand this; you just have to allow the light of the truth shine in your heart and mind – and then you *know*.

Let me conclude this chapter with these words to pique your curiosity toward that "something better" that I keep alluding to. This comes from my friend in Sydney, Australia, and the author of, *The Grand Illusion: A Synthesis of Science and Spirituality, Book One,* Brendan D. Murphy. On the very first page of the book's introduction he asks,

"Have you ever wondered what is actually real? Ever questioned whether there might be more to consciousness than solely electrochemical activity in the brain? Have you ever wondered if those strange experiences where your mind and awareness seemed to reach beyond the bounds of your cranium – or even breached the boundaries of space-time – might have been real? Do you believe that humans are capable of more than the reductionists would ask you to believe? Have you ever pondered what might happen when we die? Do you want to know the difference between believing and knowing?"

And then a few pages later, Murphy poignantly states, *"More to the point is the fact that never before have we known the collective mind to be undertaking the kind of mass awakening that now appears to be happening and gathering pace, even as I type these words."*

Chapter 12:

The Law of Attraction Revisited & Reinforced

I feel that it merits revisiting the Law of Attraction – its power, its omnipresence, its validity – its reality.

I think this is necessary because, despite the worldwide knowledge and practice of this power, there is still a vast portion of the world's population that still either has absolutely no clue about it, or still refuses to accept its validity, despite verifiable, extensive scientific proof of its existence.

For example, not long ago I had a short, but revealing conversation with a young female friend of mine. She was having a casual chat with me about a little drama going on in her life, and I simply mentioned that the Law of Attraction was at work in her situation. Whereupon she responded, "The Law of Attraction? What's that?" She simply had no clue about what it is and had never even heard about it. So, there is obviously a lot of work to be done yet in bringing the knowledge and understanding about the L.O.A. into the greater realm of the world's consciousness. There is a lot of work left by the practitioners and teachers of the Law of Attraction to help the people of the world to integrate this "greatest power in the Universe" into their daily moment-to-moment lives, with good purpose.

Why is this important? It goes back to one of the seven Universal Laws I wrote about earlier in this book, and that is the Law of Deliberate Creation. Unfortunately, without the knowledge and understanding of the L.O.A., much of the world are creators of their lives by default. In other words, for them, the Law of Attraction is still a secret, and this need not be. The vast global connecting of today's world is now positively spreading the teachings and understanding of this law and powerfully and beautifully converting a great portion of the world's population into deliberate creators, in a positive manner. When this happens there will be a powerful shift in global mass consciousness from believing that all things negative are reality, to one where all things positive, loving, healthy, and joyful are realized as true reality. To me, this would be an amazing, beautiful turning of the tide of human consciousness, and because of it, would also further contribute to an exponential increase in the rise of true spirituality. As the subtitle of this book states, it would be a further cementing of the true symbiotic relationship of the Law of Attraction and true spirituality – to the benefit of all mankind. True spirituality and the Law of Attraction share the same characteristics when and if perceived and used properly together. If you remember, I stated earlier that the Law of Attraction equals Love. So too does true spirituality equal Love.

Map of the Scale of Consciousness

On this note, it is a good idea for us to take a close look at psychiatrist, David R. Hawkins' Map of Consciousness that he developed. Hawkins did a study of applied kinesiology in which he found powerful patterns that organize human behavior. This should be interesting to us since we are delving into the unseen realm (or the "implicit" realm that physicist, David Bohm, spoke about) where all energy exists. As Hawkins explains in his book, *Power vs. Force*,

"We can intuit, then, an infinite domain of infinite potential – consciousness itself – within which there is an enormously powerful attractor field organizing all of human behavior into what is innate to 'humanness'." Within the giant attractor field are sequential fields of progressively less energy and power. These fields in turn, dominate behavior, so that definable patterns are consistent across cultures and time, throughout human history. The interactions of these variations within attractor fields make up the history of civilization and mankind."

Hawkins' scale utilizes measuring factors of consciousness such as hate, shame and humiliation at the lowest end of the scale all the way up to self-consciousness and enlightenment at the highest level of human consciousness. Along with these factors, he adds a numeric ranking from the lowest level of consciousness at 20 all the way up to 1000 at the level total enlightenment rarely, if ever, reached only by enlightened masters such as Jesus and Buddha.

Over decades of empirical research trials and studies with thousands of people, Hawkins used is kinesiology testing protocol he developed in which he claimed could infallibly tell if something was true or false, and positive, healthy, and productive, or negative, false, and destructive. Not only could his process of discerning truth from false, productive from destructive be applied to an individual via his kinesiology test, but he was able to use the same scale of consciousness on the mass consciousness of humanity.

One thing interesting that Hawkins notes is that for many centuries, the mass consciousness of humankind stayed static at the calibrated level of 190, but within the late 20th. Century jumped to 207. This is significant in that Hawkins says that the level below 200 is (as they call it in baseball, the "Mendoza Line") where negative energies and emotions exist. Above 200 is when human consciousness/your consciousness finally moves into the positive, productive realm of energy, emotion, and thought. I do believe that this jump to 207 by humankind's consciousness is an important marker that reflects the progress the population of the world is making toward awakening to all things enlightening, metaphysical, and spiritual. The most likely and powerful factor in this jump is because of the late 20th. Century spread of global connectedness and knowledge – in a way never before possible in all of history, mainly because of the internet.

The key thing to note here in studying this map of consciousness is its importance to building your rock-solid personal foundation and strong pillars. The higher up the scale of consciousness you go, the more consistent and powerful you will become as a co-creator in using the Law of Attraction. Every one of the characteristics that lie below the calibrated consciousness level of 200 are elements that will absolutely cause cracks to develop in your 3 Pillars and undermine the strength and stability of the personal foundation of your life. The beauty of Hawkins' map of consciousness is that you now have an actual scientifically proven and researched scale (Hawkins did his research over a 20 year period in which he took millions of consciousness calibrations on human test subjects) that shows you how and where you need to be to raise the strength and power of your being to live the life you love and love the life you live. This will eliminate all worrying that it will come crashing down around you and continue the seemingly endless cycle of "... from dust to dust".

Why this is important to our understanding of how to use the Law of Attraction in your life is that it relates also to its symbiotic relationship to true spirituality. Remember, practicing and living in the right-mindedness of the eternal, unchanging Universal Truths (true spirituality) will allow you to move up this scale of calibrations of human consciousness. Scientific research now backs this up. To whit in a research paper, *"Constructive and Unconstructive Repetitive Thought"* (Edward R. Watkins, 2008, University of Exeter) *"By constantly telling yourself you can achieve something, you predict a constructive outcome. Positive repetitive thought (RT) has been found to enable: (a) recovery from upsetting and traumatic events, (b) adaptive preparation and anticipatory planning, (c) recovery from depression, and (d) uptake of health-promoting behaviors."*

More Scientific Proof

Now let us again turn one more time to science to give us a powerful, true understanding of the vast, unlimited reserve of power that is at the beck and call on a moment's notice to every person on the planet via the Law of Attraction – all the while remembering that *everything is energy*.

Lynne McTaggart points out in her book, *The Field*, that,

"Every quantum physicist is well aware of the Zero Point Field. Quantum mechanics had demonstrated that there is no such thing as a vacuum, or nothingness. What we tend to think of as a sheer void if all space were emptied of matter and you examined even the space between the stars is, in subatomic terms, a hive of activity...What we believe to be our stable, static universe is in fact a seething maelstrom of subatomic particles popping in and out of existence."

So here we have scientists telling us that which we cannot see, even on cosmic terms, is real energy. Since we already understand that everything is energy, then it is easy to extrapolate this understanding just like the Law of Attraction. This bears the reiteration of the statement that once you become cognizant of the realness and power of your thoughts, then you better become aware of the what, where, and how you direct them. You are thinking and moving about in a real unseen realm of energy of which every atom of your body, and every atom of the energy of your thoughts, stir this cosmic pot of energy that you are swimming in in this exact moment.

Practical Application of the Law of Attraction

With the world of science verifying at every turn the truth and existence of the Law of Attraction and how it works, let us now turn our attention to its practical application.

In a world of creators by default, we now understand that it is not only practical, but very doable to live your life on a moment-to-moment basis as a deliberate creator. It all boils down to the knowledge you now have that very real power to create using the Law of Attraction, available to you right now. With this new knowledge of yours comes knowing that you have the power to choose your every thought, your every emotion, and point it in the direction you desire.

The way most people of the world now think, and act is as if they were a ship without a rudder. They allow every "wave" of life to knock them this way and that way seemingly without recourse. This is only because they simply don't realize that they have the power to choose what, when, where, and how their life goes. Simply by coming to this powerful understanding of their ability to choose, suddenly a rudder is added to their "ship". As I always say, the Law of Attraction is not complicated to use or understand. There is no complexity in this power of choosing. All that is involved to put it in action is to remember that you *do* have this power and always have – but somehow you forgot. I have encountered many people whereupon realizing that they are not a default creator, a victim of life, undergoing a revelation. It is like of bolt of energizing light that sweeps across their mind and being, and this is a beautiful thing to behold.

Speaking of the simplicity of using the Law of Attraction properly, there are many, many processes that are easy to integrate into your daily life. One of these processes is called "**Pivoting**".

The process of pivoting is a simple and quick way of using your power of choice in the moment. If during any of your casual thoughts or conversations, and even just dreaming or envisioning you catch yourself drifting into that realm of what you *don't* want, you on-the-spot turn your thoughts and words around 180 degrees – *pivot* – and aim their energy in the opposite direction toward what you *do* want to manifest in your life.

For example, say you catch yourself in a conversation with a co-worker that pay day is this Friday, but "All that money will be gone by the next day when I pay my bills!" The energy and direction of this statement is aimed in the direction of lack, and negativity. There is no energy of gratitude or abundance in your statement. If like attracts like (the credo of the Law of Attraction), then by *law* – Universal, all-powerful law – more of this lack and negativity will be sent to you. Now in your new understanding of how to pivot, you now consciously turn your thoughts, words, and emotions in the direction of, "I am so grateful that my paycheck supplies all the money that I need to pay all of my bills, and keep my family well fed, warm, healthy, and well cared for." By *law* more of the energy of this statement and thought *must* be sent to you. There is no complexity in this process of pivoting as you stand in your very real power to choose to be a deliberate creator of the joyful, happy, and abundant life you want.

As you do this process, at first it might be wise to keep your own counsel, as many of your family members and acquaintances may not be aligned with you on this, and still be stuck within the ego-directed, dualistic belief that "reality" (as the ego-directed world knows it) is all things bad. The classic retort from these people is "Oh man, get real, will you?" as you espouse your dreams and goals. Despite the available scientific proof of the legitimacy of the Law of Attraction, they choose to remain in their ignorance of it. If you do share this with them without knowing where they stand, then their energy and words may drag you down as they act as energy vampires.

As Baba Ram Dass once said,

"If you think you are enlightened, just try spending a weekend with your family."

Another very simple to implement Law of Attraction process is called the "**Rampage of Appreciation**". In order to do this process, you must first again remember the key understanding that *everything* is energy.

As you begin this process, you turn all of your thoughts and words to the power of your appreciation for everything in your life, and even those things that are not in your life but effect the overall quality of life in the world.

Statements of appreciation like...

- I am so grateful for the excellent health I have had my entire life!

- I appreciate the love and support that my husband/wife gives me!

- I love that I am up for consideration for the promotion at work!

- I am so grateful that my teacher was complimentary to me today about that assignment I turned in!

- I am so happy at just how pleasant and nice the recent streak of weather has been!

- We are so fortunate that the best condo at the resort in Cabo was available for us during our upcoming vacation!

These affirmative, appreciative statements of yours, of course, are nothing but pure energy, but they are vibrating at a much faster, higher frequency than any of your negative thoughts and words could ever achieve. This is important in that you have turned the dial up on the vibrational energy of your being. As you add your powerful and positive emotions to the equation and back it all up with envisioning your appreciative statements as being true, you then are well on your way to becoming that deliberate creator we have been talking so much about.

You can do this rampage of appreciation anywhere. For instance, if you are in a café reading this right now, pull out a pen, grab a couple napkins to write on, and start rampaging! Pull out your laptop and start typing, or even just start saying out loud everything you appreciate about your life right now. More of what you appreciate *must* be sent to you.

One more L.O.A. process for becoming a deliberate creator of the life you truly desire, is yet another very simple process called "**Scripting**."

I'm sure at some point in time of watching sports on television prior to the game or event, you have seen one or several of the athletes sitting with their eyes closed in a meditative style moving their head and body in synchronicity with what they are envisioning in their head. They are going through the process in their mind's eye of seeing themselves successfully, fluidly, and effortlessly performing the physical activity necessary in their sport. This is the mental version of what you need to do when you do scripting.

When you script, you sit with a piece of paper and write or type exactly how you want every single detail of what you want to manifest in your physical reality. The fun part about scripting is this is where you really start to grasp that you really *are* the sole writer, producer, and director of the movie of your life! There is real freedom in this process, as it may perhaps be the very first time in your life you have allowed your mind to flow unrestricted to the highest levels of your imagination of how you want it to be in your life. You could most likely compare it to flying – where you are high in the sky above the clouds with the sun shining radiantly upon everything as far as you can see! Up here, there really is nothing that you cannot be, do, or have – literally, even the sky is not the limit!

This is where the power of scripting comes in in that you are raising the vibrational energy of what you desire to higher and higher levels. The better and better you feel about it, the more you are magnifying the energy of it all. And as we have already seen, the better you feel, the power of your emotions increases, which raises the energy of your scripting and making it even more powerful. Once you have written the script of how you want things to unfold for yourself, take a cue from the athletes I mentioned, and then envision your script in your mind's eye in high definition to again increase its power, and align itself with the Universe for its physical manifestation in your life.

The wonderful part about using the scripting method of manifestation is that you can use it in any scenario you can imagine. For instance, next time you know that you will be sharing some time with your mom who you seem to have a difficult time agreeing with on anything, and generally getting along with, try writing out – scripting – in advance, exactly how you wish the meeting with her to go. This is the time to let go of dwelling on those things you always disagree with her on, and the anxiety of having to spend time with her. This is where you use your power as a very real creator to create how you truly want the meet-up with your mom to go! Write it out something like...

I arrive at my mom's house on time, and as soon as I get in the house, I give her a hug, but this time, it's a very real, genuine hug. I see the look of surprise on her face, but it doesn't take long before she says something that usually gets under my skin, only this time I simply shrug it off, and instead I remember that it just is not important in the grand scheme of things. She continues to say these things to me, but instead of my getting angry at her, I counter with compliments about how nice she looks today, and how clean her house looks. After a while of me staying balanced and loving, I notice a subtle shift in her continence toward me, instead of intentionally saying things to me to make me stay on edge, she too starts saying loving and kind things to me. After a half hour of this, for the first time in many years, my mom and I start to act like the buddies we were when I was a kid, and we start hashing over some of the fond memories from those times. By the time I get ready to leave, we again hug, but this time it's a real, genuine hug on both our parts. This is the best visit that my mom and I have had together in a long time, and I am genuinely looking forward to our next get together!

As you can see by doing so, scripting really is you being the writer, producer, and director of your life. Try this process, then watch how what you wrote out in your script, much to your amazement, slowly but surely unfolds in some way, shape or form in a positive manner.

There is tremendous power in the scripting process, and I can guarantee that at some point in time (possibly sooner rather than later) you will start to see and experience the positive results of your scripting.

One word of caution when using any L.O.A. process is to not try to force the Universe's hand by demanding that it deliver it to you in the exact form you desire. One of the key things you should always remember when working with the Law of Attraction is that the Universe knows way better than you just exactly how your desires and wants should be delivered to you for your greatest good, and all those concerned. This is especially true of the time frame in which it is delivered to you. It always comes to you in the right way at the right time, which quite possibly does not jive with when you *think* it should come to you.

This chapter, of course, is a review and reinforcement of the Law of Attraction, while the entire book is a treatise on the symbiotic relationship that the L.O.A. shares with true spirituality. Recently I read Lesson #253 the "Workbook for Students" section of *A Course in Miracles.* As soon as I read it, I knew that it is perhaps the best true spiritual explanation of how you truly are creator of your life, your world!

Lesson 253
My self is ruler of the universe.

It is impossible that anything should come to me unbidden by myself. Even in this world, it is I who rule my destiny. What happens is what I desire. What does not occur is what I do not want to happen. This must I accept. For thus am I led past this world to my creations, children of my will, in Heaven where my holy Self abides with them and Him Who has created me.

You are the Self Whom You created Son, creating like Yourself and one with you. My Self, Which rules the universe, is but Your Will in perfect union with my own, which can but offer glad assent to Yours, that it may be extended to Itself.

Chapter 13:

Forgiveness: Two Paths to Choose From

"The real world cannot be perceived except through eyes forgiveness blesses, so they see a world where terror is impossible and witnesses to fear cannot be found."

From the "Workbook for Students" in A Course in Miracles

So far, we've gone deep into the energetic workings of attraction and how to successfully implement it into your life. Now let us take a deeper dive into another important spiritual element involved in this beautiful symbiotic dance between the Law of Attraction and true spirituality. In the last chapter of this book we will put it all together.

Earlier in this book I touched upon what I call the "keystone" of your life, forgiveness. Following your path to forgiveness will always take you to a split in the path – one way takes you down the road that is ego directed and keeps you stuck here within the dream, and the other way leads you to true spiritual forgiveness and takes you back home into the arms of your Creator.

When the moment occurs when you need to forgive someone or something – someone stole money from you, someone beat you up, you were raped, your wife or husband asks for a divorce, etc., and you come to the forgiveness split in the road, which road will you choose?

The Forgiveness of the Ego

So, an event happened in your life that harmed you in some way physically, mentally, financially, relationally, and you can't decide whether to take revenge or forgive, but if you decide to take the high road – the spiritual road, the choice must always be to forgive. However, herein lies the danger of making the wrong choice.

If you choose to forgive as the world has chosen to for all of history, then you walk the path of the ego's forgiveness. Forgiveness as practiced by the ego/the world, *always* stems from your perception that the harm done to you came from outside yourself, from another source other than you. It is based in the ego's religion of separation. As the ego would have you forgive, it chants the mantra, "It's not my fault!" However, as we have learned as true spiritual students, anything and everything that happens to you was projected by you to create the world you see and perceive. If you follow the path of practicing forgiveness as the world uses it (as a form of attack), you may think you are hurting that person or thing, but in reality, you are attacking and hurting yourself. In doing so this is like adding yet another layer of hurt upon the hurt you perceived as being perpetrated against you and adding even more pain to it all. This is a difficult thing to understand or believe, but as you continue your studies of true spirituality, the dark, false thoughts will vaporize as the Light of your Source takes their place with very real unconditional love.

There is another aspect to consider in your practice of forgiveness, and that is the matter of karma. Karma is ancestral and past lives works that are low energy, negative experiences and situations that are carried on into your other lives and may even have been energetically bequeathed to you from one of your ancestors. According to many spiritual and shamanic teachings, each of us carries seven generations worth of karma within each of our lifetimes. This is a very heavy load for anyone to bear, especially when you realize that almost all of it is out of your conscious realm buried deep in your subconscious. With this understanding, again we see that once this knowledge dawns upon your conscious mind, it becomes easier to see how practicing quantum forgiveness has merit to no end.

In the book, *The Second Wave: Transcending the Human Drama* by Kerri Hummingbird and White Eagle there is a section by Akashic channeler and the founder of the Akashic School of Wisdom, Lisa Barnett. In this section Barnett refers to the Akashic Record Keepers from throughout time that, "*The Record Keepers also tell us that the easiest way to clear karma is through forgiveness. When we can forgive the soul, who is also a being of light on a journey, you can then move into compassion and love, which will release old karma throughout time.*"

You can see that without the knowledge that true spirituality gives you to help you finally break through that worldly crust and dogma that has formed over your heart and mind. It can be close to impossible to understand how and why you can practice and live with true forgiveness as a clearing tool that allows you to see the light of true spirituality. What makes it even harder is that if you have up to seven generations of karma to carry around with you, the burden of it all can be a load too heavy to carry by yourself. This is why some people just continue to carry on the same old addictions and negative beliefs, thoughts, and actions that have plagued their family line for centuries. It could also be why some people commit suicide. They have no access to the light beyond their generational karma and end their life not even understanding why – they just can't take it anymore because it is simply unbearable.

This is the path the ego wants you to go down the path of continued darkness and separation that leads to yet another and then another and then another cycle of bad karma. The ego is *not* your friend, and only wants your destruction so the perpetual cycle of attack, murder, and judgment continues generation after generation. The ego gains power and extends its lifespan by keeping you in the separate-from-your- Source mode. The only way out of this perpetual cycle is your practice of true, quantum forgiveness.

Definition of True or Quantum Forgiveness

Let us once again take a look at what true forgiveness is, or as I like to refer to is as Quantum Forgiveness.

True spiritual forgiveness is one of equality, where all is recognized as one without separation. Whatever seemed to happen to you to make you perceive that a wrong was done to you is really just an illusion. It didn't really happen! You now understand that this life of yours and the world around you that you perceive is only a dream while you, the Son of God, is asleep within a tiny mad idea of separation. This makes any perceived attack upon you not real, so there really is nothing to forgive. With this knowing, the unity and oneness of All-That-Is is undisturbed, and you move forth on your journey ensconced in only unconditional love where there is and never will be anything to forgive.

With this definition of quantum forgiveness in your heart, and your continued practice of it, all bad karma and all akashic records simply fall away.

As Buddha says, *"I cannot forgive you because I have no grudge against you."*

And...

"To understand everything is to forgive everything."

Forgiveness & Retribution: The Human-Forged, Non-Symbiotic Relationship

To think that one can speak the words "forgiveness" and "retribution" in the same sentence is ludicrous at best. Speaking these two words in the same sentence actually cancels out the meaning of the word "forgiveness" as we would like to think about it. It is well understood that when light enters the darkness, darkness is immediately dispelled, however in this case when retribution enters forgiveness' space, darkness immediately dispels the light. While the existence of light can never be obliterated, only obscured, retribution simply causes light to move into the realm of the unseen, thus unperceived. Never can the two legitimately dwell together in the same space.

When we forgive, we would like to think and believe that we have let go of something or someone who has committed a wrong against us. The "let go of" means that it no longer has any influence over your thoughts, words, actions, and emotions simply because it is no longer a part of your life and experience – you've let-it-GO!

Unfortunately, this is simply not how the majority of the population of the world practices forgiveness. As the world practices it, the words forgiveness and retribution become synonymous. The reason for this is that the teachings of the world are forged in ego-based duality. For every wrong action, retribution or punishment is merited, and must be doled out.

Just look at the justice system in most any court in the world, where the face of forgiveness rarely gets even a nod or a smile of recognition. A recent experience in the United States in which potential jurors were undergoing questioning to see if they would be selected, one person responded to the judge's question by saying, "I am a firm believer in true spiritual forgiveness, and if I am selected to sit on the jury, no matter what the charges against the defendant, my response will never be 'guilty or innocent', but only and always, 'I forgive you'". Whereupon the judge and the attorneys were observed scribbling furiously in their note pads. Needless to say, this person was *not* selected as one of the jurors for the case. No matter where in the world a courtroom exists, forgiveness is rarely, if ever, invited in.

Let us look at exactly how the world's egoic form of forgiveness works based on the duality of separation.

The world's form of forgiveness is one based on inequality. A person experiences and perceives a wrong that has been done to them by a person or group, and even an animal, and then says, "I forgive you". The words have been spoken, however the victim who spoke the words of forgiveness does not erase the ingrained thought that something hurtful happened to them, and even though they say the word "forgive", in her heart and mind it is an unmerited forgiveness. The victim of the hurt sits on a higher platform of judgment looking down at the perpetrator who now remains on a lower level because they did something bad. This will remain so literally forever in the heart and mind of the victim unless some form of catharsis occurs to release the hurt to true forgiveness – and even a catharsis is no guarantee that this will take place. The ego's version of unequal and separate forgiveness has a strong grip.

And if you are surprised that this egoic form of human forgiveness can extend even to animals, one need look no further than any incident in which a wild animal, following its natural instincts, attacks and harms a person, retribution is almost always the answer by the hunting down and killing of the attacking animal. This is yet another example of retribution blotting out any light forgiveness has to offer.

The reverberation of the human dualistic, ego-based form of forgiveness will forever echo in a continuous loop, "You hurt me! I am 'up here', and you are bad and are 'down there' in my eyes forever – *but I forgive you.*"

And the egoic form of human forgiveness is perpetually reinforced in today's high-tech world of instantaneous communication via the internet, and all forms of media entertainment and news.

Take a moment to review the latest movies you see or in the entertainment section of any newspaper in the world. There are countless movies and television shows whose main theme is that of retribution and vengeance. The main plot always seems to be that some form of brutal and deadly hurt was doled out to an individual or the individual's family, and the rest of the entire show follows the "hero" as they kill, maim, and injure everyone they see as responsible for this awful hurt. "Screw the forgiveness! Kill them all!" screams each and every one of these forms of "entertainment", all the while reinforcing the way the world continues to practice forgiveness (or lack thereof).

As for the news programs on television, once a report of some wrong-doing by an individual or group comes on, and the way it is presented, the human mind almost always jumps immediately into a form of egoic judgement that screams – "GUILTY!" – instead of what should be the assumption of "innocent until proven guilty". There is rarely if ever a modicum of forgiveness in these media reports or wrong-doing – the human ego mind will *not* allow it!

At some point, somewhere, somehow, someone has to stand up and shout at the top of their voice from the highest mountain – *"ENOUGH ALREADY! STOP!"*

There is a form of forgiveness that I previously mentioned where forgiveness and retribution shall never, ever meet, and that is *Quantum Forgiveness*. It is worthy of further study.

Quantum forgiveness has been around for much of human history but only within a very few religions such as Buddhism and Hinduism in which the dualism of the ego enters not. Instead, it is understood that the reality of human existence is based only in unity and oneness. In the late 20th century and now in the early 21st century, this is being taught and expounded by *A Course in Miracles*, which is based on the teaching of pure, uncompromising, non-dualistic unity and oneness of all creatures and things. In the practice of quantum forgiveness, no inequality exists, nor can it exist. If it does, then it again becomes dualistic in nature, based upon separation.

This explanation obviously is hard for the world's ego to swallow because it exposes the truth of how the world practices forgiveness by replacing it with retribution, inequality, and separation. This explanation of quantum forgiveness may also trigger the "woo" factor with most of the world in that they inherently think it is all mumbo-jumbo. However, it has already been proven scientifically that we – everything – is a matrix of interconnectedness of All-That-Is, or as author, Lynne McTaggart, refers to it in her book, *The Field,* as the "Zero Point Field".

In her book she speaks of numerous research projects on the human brain and behavior done by famed 20th century psychologist, Karl Pribam, and many other prominent and respected scientists and researchers, it is stated, *"The fact that the human body was exchanging information with a mutable field of quantum fluctuation suggested something profound about the world. It hinted at human capabilities for knowledge and communication far deeper and more extended than we presently understand. It also blurred the boundary lines of our individuality – our very sense of separateness. If living things boil down to charged particles interacting with a field and sending out and receiving quantum information, where did we end and the rest of the world begin? Where was consciousness – encased inside our bodies or out there in The Field? Indeed, there was no more 'out there' if we and the rest of the world were so intrinsically interconnected."*

This is just one step toward slamming the door on the "woo" factor. There are numerous verified scientific research projects published in the most respected scientific journals of our time and performed by some of the most brilliant scientists in the world. Each of these projects confirms the intimate, innate interconnectedness of every individual who has ever existed throughout human history, into a very real oneness and collective consciousness that is necessary to practice quantum forgiveness.

For further scientific research as proof of the oneness of all that encompasses our universe, one need look no further than Brendan D. Murphy's voluminous book, *The Grand Illusion: A Synthesis of Science and Spirituality, Book One*, in which he speaks about the ground breaking work of Quantum Physicist, David Bohm.

"Bohm called our everyday world of space, time, and causality the 'explicate order'. He proposed that underlying this world is the 'implicate order', from which our manifest reality is projected (literally, unfolds)."

And Murphy goes on to cite...

"Perennial Philosophy (the philosophical tradition of the world's great thinkers dealing with problems of ultimate reality as the nature of being) *offers the philosophical background most consistent with the new scientific paradigm...What remains after you subtract state, time, and culture-dependent realities, which are all transient 'inventions', is the unbroken, unified, and eternal consciousness that creates and pervades all. This realization is at the core of all major religions (behind the exoteric dogmas), and incidentally, is also the view of various 'spiritual' physicists, who see what quantum physics is pointing us towards."*

As the title of Murphy's book suggests, over the last century or more, there really has been a synthesis of science and spirituality, with the scientists now saying what the spiritual icons have been saying for thousands of years, only using different lingo to describe the same thing – We are all one, and separation of anything does not and cannot exist! And as noted in the above quote that the original core teachings of all major religions are obscured by their exoteric dogmas, which is why today's organized religions will never be able to practice unconditional or quantum forgiveness.

Despite the scientific proof of universal oneness which allows one to understand that any conditional forgiveness is all the world can ever offer, the vast majority of the world's populace keeps its blinders in place and refuses to accept the obvious. Because of this, in truth, the "woo" factor falls squarely on the unbelievers of the truth of oneness – a oneness that makes valid the statement, "As you do unto others, so shall you do unto yourself."

Quantum or true spiritual forgiveness flies squarely in the face of the human ego who is determined to keep world's conditional forgiveness tied to retribution so that it may remain strong and powerful via the resulting conflict, human drama, and hate. The beautiful thing is that the mind of the world is awakening to what true spiritual forgiveness is at a geometrically increasing pace, so that one day the light of understanding and very real, unencumbered forgiveness will soon become our human reality.

"Can you imagine how beautiful those you forgive will look to you? In no fantasy have you ever seen anything so lovely. Nothing you see here, sleeping or waking, comes near to such loveliness. And nothing will you value like unto this, nor hold so dear."

-A Course In Miracles, TX-17.I.1.

Chapter 14:

Catharsis & Catastrophe: Are They Necessary for Spiritual Advancement?

"Fear binds the world. Forgiveness sets it free."
Lesson #332, A Course in Miracles

Now we come to a chapter of this book that I really would rather not have to write, but it is a topic that we must take an in depth look at – the roles of catharsis and catastrophe in our spiritual awakening and forgiveness lessons.

Definition of Catharsis:

1a : purification or purgation of the emotions (such as pity and fear) primarily through art
b : a purification or purgation that brings about spiritual renewal or release from tension
2 : elimination of a complex by bringing it to consciousness and affording it expression

Definition of Catastrophe

1: a momentous tragic event ranging from extreme misfortune to utter overthrow or ruin. Deforestation and erosion can lead to an ecological catastrophe.
2: utter failure : fiasco//the party was a catastrophe
3a: a violent and sudden change in a feature of the earth
b: a violent usually destructive natural event (such as a supernova)
4: the final event of the dramatic action especially of a tragedy

As mentioned, I am loath to have to write about these two words, and how they play a part in each of our lives during our journey in human form. Unfortunately, it seems that far too many people are hard-wired from birth to meet head on with some form of catharsis and/or catastrophe at some point in their life. And, of course, many times the two seem to come together.

The understanding of catharsis and catastrophe became particularly poignant during the year 2020 with the global spread of a virus known as the corona virus or its medical title COVID-19 (which stands for the year 2019 in which it was discovered, its "novel" status, and the name of the virus family, CoV, from which it comes from).

The appearance and spread of this virus became, perhaps for the very first time ever, a catastrophe of true global proportions. Because of the ease of intercontinental travel (in which people are packed closely together on an airplane), and the worldwide knowledge of the situation communicated almost instantaneously by the lightning quick global connectedness via the internet and modern electronic communications. Literally every country – superpowers on down to tiny third world countries – stopped almost all human interaction, specifically incorporating something called "social distancing", to avoid the spread of this bacteria. For the first time in recorded human history, the entire world shut down almost completely as a unit. Race, socioeconomic status, religion, and creed mattered not, as this virus was indiscriminate in who it attacked regardless of their place in the world. Consequently, fear spread like wildfire and grew more widespread within the world's mass consciousness. Truly the world had never experienced anything so globally pervasive, and the human race as a whole was sent scrambling to enforce any seemingly appropriate measures to stifle the advance of the virus. It was an unprecedented, supposedly unexpected event – or was it?

We established very early in this book that thoughts are very real energy. This is true not only of the thoughts of each individual, but the thoughts of all beings on earth as a unit.

From the book, *Seth Speaks: The Eternal Validity of the Soul* by Jane Roberts, Seth (the etheric entity that Roberts channeled into multiple books over a period of years) states, *"Every thought that you have now changes reality. Not only reality as you know it, but all reality."* If this is true, which I believe it is, imagine that for you as an individual, how much more the thought of the human mass consciousness must have unimaginable power and influence over all that manifests and occurs in our world! This is an excellent example of the Law of Attraction working on the mass consciousness of humanity. You now literally have an entire planet of billions of people focusing a singular thought of "I do not want to get this virus!" gripped in the vice of the powerful emotion of fear and thoughts of separation. This is massive energetic attraction on a global scale so powerful that the Law of Attraction can only continue to send more and more for the world to be afraid of. It produces a snowball effect as when you roll a snowball down a snowy hill, and it keeps getting larger and larger it has reached the size of a boulder at the hill's bottom.

In saying that no one could have possibly predicted the global-wide catastrophe of the spread of the COVID-19 virus in 2020, I think would be a great disservice to the true power and nature of the very real energy of thought, especially on the scale of the mass of all humanity. (The Law of Attraction at work riding the massive wave of the negative, low vibrating energy of fear being produced all at once by all of humanity – like attracts more of the same.)

While ecologists have spoken for years on the negative effect of climate change, pollution, and overpopulation. Spiritualists, and empaths have been pointing to signs and effects of the negative, low vibrating energy of the world's mass consciousness for a very long time. They will all tell you that the dark energy of global thoughts does have and has had an effect on Mother Earth far in advance of the first globally acknowledged catastrophic spread of this virus. Wildfires have been raging for many years throughout the world, and have increased in intensity and their reach, every bit as indiscriminate as the virus itself. In 2019 and into early 2020 wildfires raged in much of the state of California in the United States, and seemingly engulfed much of the country of Australia. The results of these fires were nothing short of brutal. Meteorologists will tell you that over the last few years they have never seen anything like the epidemic of hurricanes and typhoons that have ravaged much of the world. Never before in recorded history has there been such a consistent rash of violent storms. And when it comes to sicknesses like the spread of COVID-19, SARS, Ebola, H.I.V., and infulenza, when one is seemingly tamed or cured, yet another deadly bacterium pops up to take its place.

All these destructive entities are a symptom of the low vibrating, negative, dark energy of mass thought, which has for most of history dwelled in the realm of fear. This consistent residency of human thought within the realm of fear reached a frenzied peak on a global scale during the COVID-19 virus pandemic, and according to the Law of Attraction, that which you think and dwell upon, more of that will be sent to you by the universe. Remembering the quote above from Seth, *"Every thought that you have now changes reality. Not only reality as you know it, but all reality"* which means that this worldwide mass consciousness of fear becomes unimaginably powerful in producing more to fear.

From an online blog entitled *Natural Disasters and the Law of Attraction* by New York City physician, Dr. Kulkani, she states, *"Mass events, like a hurricane, aren't the result of one person's energy – they are the result of a collective mass consciousness, which gains its own momentum."* So, like the global mass consciousness of intense fear of dying from a virus, more to be afraid of in the form of more viruses and other disasters and human conflict are then attracted into the physical reality of mankind.

Further proof that focused thought energy of a large number of people (thus invoking the Law of Attraction) can have a positive, peaceful result comes from a 1993 meditation experiment. A two-month national demonstration project that took place in Washington, D.C., showed how a group of meditators can reduce crime and social stress. This was a carefully controlled scientific demonstration carried out between June 7 and July 30, 1993. The study involved a coherence group of transcendental meditators who increased in number from 800 to a maximum of 4,000 over the trial. This group meditating crime prevention project in Washington showed a maximum 23.3% reversal in the predicted violent crime trend. Before the project, violent crime had been steadily increasing during the first five months of the year. When the project disbanded crime in the Washington D.C. area began to rise again. In the end, the maximum decrease was 23.3% below the time series prediction for that period of the year. This significant reversal in the predicted crime trend occurred when the size of the group was at its largest in the final week of the project

We've already established that via science and the spiritual teachers of all of history that everything is energy, and everything is connected (The Field). This knowledge negates any of the naysayers still stuck in the realm of Newtonian physics that all these natural and unnatural disasters come strictly from natural physical causes. The *real* cause of the dramatic buildup of catastrophes is the low vibrating, dark energy of the world's mass consciousness. If you remember Dr. David Hawkins' chart of calibrated consciousness of humankind, he asserted that the consciousness of most of the population of the world has for most of history registered below the level of 200 – a great indicator that the world's thoughts were not even remotely close to any form of enlightenment. Over and over both science and spiritual leaders have shown us that the world we see, and experience is that which we project from our mind and perceive in our visual reality as hard matter.

Lesson #325 from the *Workbook for Students* in *A Course in Miracles* gets straight to the point on this matter.

"All things I think I see reflect ideas."

As it turned out with the virus pandemic ("pandemic" – an epidemic of panic/fear – *my definition*) of 2020, the ego used its brilliant but insidious ruse to grow stronger, and more powerful, and became massively energized. It feeds off human fear, drama, and conflict, which now encompassed the entire population of earth. The worst part about the ego's seeming victory over man was that on a global basis, it drove a wedge between the billions of individuals on the planet to solidify the belief that we really are only a body and completely and totally separate from each other. This is a wedge that will take a long time to overcome, and was comprised of the thought, "If I touch this person, I *could die!"* A devious plan of separation that seemingly worked to perfection. And even what was once considered insane suddenly became sane. Germophobes, people who are obsessive compulsive in observing every facet of hygiene to avoid contact with germs of any kind, who were once considered to be border line insane, now all of a sudden became the sane ones! All the cleansing rituals that they obsessively observed, now became the norm for all of society in all countries in the world. Now what had been considered insane was now the norm for all the world! The COVID-19 pandemic caused a massive perspective shift from what was considered to be insane to now be sane! It was a catharsis of hygiene.

Consequently, for a long time afterward, hugging, and even shaking hands became things of the distant past. The ego had done its job (using fear implanted in every individual's mind) in solidifying the paradigm that we are all separate, and must stay separate, especially if we did not want to die from an infectious disease. Similar to the post 9/11 world, the world as we knew it had dramatically, in almost overnight fashion, lost much of its innocence and much of its personal freedom, too. It became a world where fear and panic dominated the mass consciousness and was then projected outward resulting visual "reality" of more fear and panic.

Quantum physics has scientifically proven that the simple act of observing something *changes* the outcome and/or characteristics of that which is being observed! If you are observing something that you think is fearful (i.e., a virus and its effects), the simple act of your observation *makes* it something to be fearful. In consideration of the incredible power of the collective consciousness of humankind, observing a particular thing such as the threat of a virus, as fearful, magnifies it into a super powerful fear – this time on a global scale! This is yet another verification of the omnipresence of the Law of Attraction's "like attracts like".

If this is the role of catastrophe with the human mind, what role does catharsis play?

According to the above definition, catharsis is a purging or purifying that brings about spiritual renewal or a release of tension (usually both). This catharsis is usually a result of some form of catastrophe. While we usually think of this happening on the individual scale, catharsis, while seemingly rare, can also occur on the worldwide scale within mass consciousness. Why is this important to understand as we delve into this topic of the synthesis of true spirituality and the Law of Attraction? At this point in human history some form of catharsis, either of the individual, and more importantly of the collective consciousness of all of mankind, is needed!

Let us go back to Dr. David Hawkins' testimonial of his enduring catharsis of spiritual awakening and awareness occurring because of his almost freezing to death as a youngster in a deadly cold, raging winter snowstorm (a catastrophe). This is a perfect example of a catharsis that resulted in a completely different perspective of his perceived reality within the spiritual realm. Catharsis really *is* a form of purging of the old, and the coming in of the new. The new usually is in a form of something usually perceived as being better, and utterly different from what was perceived before. It is a classic example of the dark being replaced by the light; the false being replaced by the truth; the ego's illusions replaced by the Truth of All-That-Is, by God.

It is my hope that a catharsis of hope and light, a global spiritual awakening, occurs in every mind of man, whether it because of the 2020 COVID-19 pandemic, or some other tragedy. Now here's the beautiful part when considering the effects of a catastrophe(s) and the resulting catharsis – *it doesn't have to happen this way!* Why? Because at every moment of your life you have free will to choose – to make the choice of right-minded spiritual truth that is based in the non-dualistic reality of eternal, unconditional love and forgiveness. And when you make this right-minded choice, no matter what the seeming catastrophe or tragedy, all fear disappears, and only love remains.

Once again, *A Course in Miracles*, comforts us in reminding us that,

---

"I gladly make the sacrifice of fear...And as we pay the debt we owe the truth – a debt which merely is the letting-go of self-deceptions and of images we worshipped falsely – truth returns to us in

wholeness and in joy. We are deceived no longer. Love has now returned to our awareness. And we are at peace again, for fear has gone and only love remains."

-Lesson #323

Although I may make it look like catastrophe and catharsis are attached at the hip, I believe that catharsis – *"a purging of negative, unproductive emotions, thoughts and beliefs that brings a release and renewal mainly in the mental/ spiritual realm"*, can take place without a catastrophe happening. However, unfortunately, it seems that that is what it usually takes to shock one out of the rut or negative spiral downward one is stuck in – a shock to your system – in order to have a revelation. A catharsis opens your inner eye to things you were blind to before, things that were unseen in the spectrum of your human vision, but all of a sudden you have become aware of. And again, the reason a catharsis does not have to be accompanied by a tragedy is because you have the free will to choose! You can wait until a catastrophe happens to you to cause that shift, or consciously *choose* now to make this cathartic shift without the catastrophic trauma. Simply put, the choice is yours!

In a reflection of the negative, destructive mindset of most of the people on the planet, in his book, *Sick Souls, Healthy Minds: How William James Can Save Your Life*, author, John Kaag, says, *"If one looks carefully, suffering is not the exception but the rule."* But on the subject of free will, Kaag quotes early 20th century philosopher and psychologist, William James. *"My first act of free will shall be to believe in free will."*

The most common belief that a catharsis usually occurs like a lightning bolt epiphany, but that is not necessarily so. In my own life, I can confidently say that most of the cathartic events in my life have been more like slowly awakening from a deep sleep in the morning. You slowly open your eyes from your slumber, and gradually perceive the first rays of light of the new day sneaking through the window blinds of your bedroom. You rub the cobwebs of sleep from your eyes, and more and more the light of the new day grows brighter until finally you become fully awake and aware of your surroundings. Consequently, any nightmares or bad dreams that you had while sleeping vaporize back into the nothingness from which they came. This is the form of catharsis/epiphany that I have experienced, slowly but surely, sometimes over the course of years. Finally, I became awake to what I had previously been unaware of, either visually, mentally, or spiritually.

This is exactly the process of atonement (undoing) and awakening God is doing with you as you slumber within your dream of separation from Him. As I touched on in Chapter 11, it is worth again noting that if He suddenly shook you as hard as He could, and screamed intensely, "WAKE UP!", the shock to your system would be too great to handle, and harm might to come to you. You would not reawaken safely and lovingly in His arms in a happy, coherent manner. Instead, He whispers quietly in your ear "Wake up my son. It is only a dream you are having." All the while gently stroking your hair and watching over you without fail to keep you safe from harm.

I believe that this is a beautiful, freeing thought that you can live your entire life without having to undergo some sort of catastrophe to awaken from your spiritual slumber. And yes, many cathartic experiences do take place almost instantaneously as the result of a catastrophic kick-in-the-butt, but you can choose for it not to be that way.

In consideration of the fact that you have free will to make the choice to skip some or any form of catastrophe during your lifetime and go straight to your enlightenment and awakening, is wonderful. However, everyone comes into this body having chosen the path of their life before their birth, and that path may include some form of disaster or tragedy. This is because in their other lifetimes, the forgiveness lessons that are necessary on their journey to their awakening of the Truth, have not yet been completed. As Seth states in his book with author, Jane Roberts, "*You have made appointments each of you, that you have forgotten. They were signed, so to speak, before you were born in this existence.*" In other words, many people have decided before they were born to come into a body, knowing that they will die in a car wreck, drown in the ocean, contract a deadly disease, or appear in a deformed body (but this knowledge stays buried deep in their unconscious). As Seth notes that "you have forgotten", yet prior to birth you decided that in this lifetime it would be your forgiveness lesson as you journey toward your ultimate awakening.

Another example of foregoing an unnecessary catastrophe during your lifetime comes from Gary Renard's book, *The Disappearance of the Universe*, in which he has a conversation with his ascended masters, Arten and Pursah, in which he was complaining to them that he had gone to the movie theatre the other day, only to waste two hours of his time watching a crappy movie. Whereupon they replied to Gary, "*No Gary, there was a reason you chose to stay and see that movie. For if you had left without staying to watch it, you would've been in a bad car accident. Gary responded, "You're kidding me, right?*" and then was informed that it was a forgiveness lesson he no longer needed to learn.

This is an excellent example of how a catastrophe can be avoided by having already walked the path of many forgiveness lessons in your other lifetimes, and another is no longer necessary. The fact remains, however, that your conscious mind is not even aware of this fact, and you just think that is was just another day in your life, yet you decided on this trajectory prior to your birth.

The Importance of Your 3 Pillars – Now, More Than Ever

As I stated in my introduction, this book is a vastly expanded version of my original eBook, *The 3 Pillars: A Simple 3 Step Process to Manifest Positive & Permanent Change in Your Life*. With our look at the roles of catharsis and catastrophe in helping you to forgive all error and awaken from your dream of separation, we can now look at The 3 Pillars as a way to bypass catastrophe and tragedy and go directly to your goal of awakening back in your home in Heaven.

I would hope by now with all we have examined, that it is obvious just *why* strengthening your mental, physical, and spiritual pillars to stand for the ages; why building your life, your personal foundation, on the rock-solid foundation of right-minded, eternal, non-dualistic principles, is so very important. In standing in the strength of your life, your rock-solid house, you become unassailable, or as *A Course in Miracles* puts it, you become invulnerable to when the ego comes pounding on your door in the attack mode. This is because you did not build your foundation on ever-shifting sand, and your pillars have no cracks in them keeping the structure/your life, standing upright.

It's like the old child's story of the 3 Little Pigs and the Big Bad Wolf (and really a child's perceptual analogy of Matthew 7:24 – 27 noted at the start of chapter 11).

Each little pig had built their own house with the first pig building his from straw, and the second pig built his home from sticks. In other words, neither of their homes were constructed of solid materials and stood on a poor foundation. Whereupon when the Big Bad Wolf came calling, he quickly and easily blew down both of their homes, and unfortunately for the pigs, they both became a meal for the wolf. But the third Little Pig built his house of brick, based on a rock-solid foundation, and when the wolf appeared, he said,

"Little pig, little pig, let me come in."
Whereupon the Little Pig said,
"No, no, by the hair on my chinny chin chin."
And the Big Bad Wolf responded,
"Then I'll huff, and I'll puff, and I'll blow your house in."

I'm sure you know the outcome of this part of the story – nothing happened! Blow as hard as he could, the wolf could not bring down the third pig's "brick-solid" home and went off looking for yet another easy meal living on a shaky foundation.

Laugh if you wish to at the childlike simplicity of this story, but it aptly demonstrates that living your life on very real spiritual principles so that you may live safely and happily during your lifetime without enduring some form of catastrophe – a catastrophe that may have been mandated when you came into form to teach you forgiveness, to teach you love, and to finally allow you to awaken from the dream, softly, gently, beautifully.

And if catharsis should come your way at this point, more than likely it will show up as a gentle, warm breeze that releases you from the close-minded, unforgiving clutches of the Big Bad Wolf – the ego.

At this point in time in the history of mankind, it should be very obvious that we are on a trajectory of global catastrophe, and we have been for a very long time. Mother Earth has put up with a lot of crap from mankind, especially in the last two centuries, and has been trying to tell us for a very long time that we are on a path to self-destruction. With Earth's ability to flex her muscles via geographical, medical, and meteorological disasters, we should know that she will not allow us to destroy her. She will take us down before she allows us to take her down the road to oblivion, the path of no return. She's certainly done this before to civilizations that threatened her. If we wish to avoid disasters of global proportions, then it's time for mankind to consciously align itself with the eternal spiritual principles I write about in these pages. In doing so we will align ourselves with Gaia and return to living in harmony with nature. The wisdom of native cultures and spiritual practices of aligning and respecting the Earth will come into full view and appreciation when we choose to take this path. If we wish to avoid disasters with global consequences, the human race must enact the Law of Attraction by joining together in harmony and alignment of loving, healing, and unifying thought. In doing so, mankind has the opportunity to create an incredibly powerful, singular, cohesive thought that can save Mother Earth, and itself as well. The beautiful symbiotic relationship of true spirituality and the Law of Attraction are the saving grace for our world and its people.

Chapter 15:

Remembering Your True Self

"But it is through knowing who you are not that the greatest obstacle to truly knowing yourself is removed."

-Eckart Tolle, A New Earth: Awakening to Your Life's Purpose

As of the year 2020, the total number of people populating the planet earth was closing in on 8 billion. That's 8,000,000,000 humans on one planet! The scary thing about this fact is not the number of people, but the fact that the vast majority these 8 billion minds identify almost exclusively with the ego's thought system. This, unfortunately, is just the way the world operates, and has done so throughout all the history of humankind. Obviously, the job of helping as many of you to remember the truth of who you really are is a gargantuan task, but not impossible. There are a growing number of spiritual students and teachers, and seekers of the truth – the *real* truth about yourself – that are working harder than ever to bring the light back into your memory.

Even with this ray of hope, at this point in time in human history, the collective consciousness of the majority reflects the ego's thought system, and as author Eckhart Tolle poignantly states in his book, *A New Earth*,

"Recognize the ego for what it is: a collective dysfunction, the insanity of the human mind."

Throughout history enlightened teachers have stated very clearly that most of the world qualifies as being insane. The evidence of this lies in looking back through history as civilization after civilization after civilization met its end and adhered to the inevitable "ashes to ashes, dust to dust" syndrome, as it was ground into the earth's crust never to be remembered. Even worse, the lessons of their demise remain mostly unlearned by future generations. Even when I was a young student of 13 years old, I remember once talking to my school counselor and asking him, "Why do we have to study history?" whereupon his response was, "I suppose it is, so we learn the lessons of our past mistakes, and create a better world." Even at that young age I somehow knew his answer was blatantly naïve and not even remotely connected to the truth that society *never* learns the lessons of its mistakes of its history! And how can it? The ego is very diligent of making sure that it is the winners of the wars that write the history books and is almost never even remotely close to the truth.

Who is the real you?

As Didymus Judas Thomas – St. Thomas – wrote in his original gospels that were discovered in a cave in 1945 in Nag Hammadi, he quotes Jesus.

"The Kingdom of the Father is spread out upon the earth, and people do not see it."

In the words of Jesus, Heaven is right here amongst us, but we are blind to it because of the veil of forgetfulness of being born into a body conceived in the paradigm of separateness and the ongoing deceit of the ego.

In light of this (or should I say in the dark of this?), it should come as no surprise that we cannot remember our own divine origin. However, there is hope! Remembering that you have the free will to choose the truth over the false, Gary Renard's Ascended Master, Arten, tells us in, *The Disappearance of the Universe*,

---

"You must learn to choose between the Holy Spirit, Who represents the real you, and the part of your mind that represents the false you."

The truth is that you are a divine being, the Holy Son of God Himself, dreaming you are in a body, separate from God, in a seemingly endless spiral of insanity and guilt, afraid of the wrath of God. *But* your eyes can be opened by making the choice of the Holy Spirit, and legitimately remembering you actually are at home in Heaven with your Father *now.*

"Know what is in front of your face, and what is hidden from you will be disclosed to you. For there is nothing hidden that will not be revealed."
Jesus, from the original Gospel of St. Thomas

And you simply cannot do both – live with both the ego and God as your masters. If you attempt to do so, St. Thomas goes on to quote Jesus,

"A person cannot mount two horses or bend two bows. And a servant cannot serve two masters, or that servant will honor the one and offend the other."

And more wise words on this topic from Arten in *Disappearance of the Universe*,

"...try to remember that everything you behold in the universe of perception has one of two purposes for you to choose from. One purpose will keep you a prisoner; the other will free you."

Since I promote building your life on a rock-solid foundation based on the right-minded thinking and choices of the eternal universal truths supported by three structurally sound pillars, serving two masters is sure to bring your house down into the dust it came from. It's a classic case of a house divided.

It's interesting to see the real truth printed in black and white but taking the action of incorporating it into your life and wrapping your arms, mind, and heart around it is where the light of the truth shines upon you assuring that your house, your life – your true Self as the Holy Son of God, will stand for all eternity.

Even as I write these words, I can sense that even just mentioning the names of Jesus and the Holy spirit makes some of you recoil in a reaction that says, "Oh no! More religious evangelism!" Well, take a deep breath and let it out, because I can assure you that in no way, shape or form does this have anything to do with religious doctrine or evangelizing. When Jesus walked the earth as a man, there was no such thing as Christianity. Man made that up long after Jesus had returned home to His Father. Yes, Jesus was a rabbi, but his teachings were that of pure spirituality without attachment to any religious dogma. Even though he was a rabbi of the Jewish faith, He certainly did not adhere to the doctrine that was taught. Jesus taught only love. There was a reason why the Jewish clergy wanted to have Jesus eliminated.

Don't let your knee-jerk reaction to organized religion keep you from the truth of who you really are – the Holy Son of God Himself. And yes, for many, this is a hard concept to accept. This is because most of us, again, have been groomed from birth to not feel worthy of such lofty thoughts; to feel guilty and separate from God, and to fear the wrath of God who wants to kill you because you had the nerve to think you could escape Him. But this is what this writing is about, helping you to finally free yourself from these false beliefs, and remember that God, our Father, is an all-loving Father, who would never cause His creation (you) any harm. He only wants you back at home with Him in Heaven where unconditional Love reigns for all of eternity. And this can happen when you make the choice to remember who you *really* are.

Make no mistake that whatever religious tradition you grew up with, no matter what country you are from, no matter what race you are, the Father awaits your remembrance and awakening. As we know too, the name of God, a Supreme Being, our Creator, comes in thousands of different names, but referring to the same entity. In Native American spiritual practice, it is the Great Spirit, in Islam it is Allah, Judaism it's Yahweh, Shiva in Hinduism, in Sikhism it is Akal Murat, and many, many, many more incarnations. I remember hearing Dr. Wayne Dyer once point out that even the "ah" sound is almost universal in all the different name's religions have created to represent the Supreme Being. This is a great example of the commonality and oneness of our being, no matter our life circumstances and standing.

Practical Ways of Remembering Your True Self

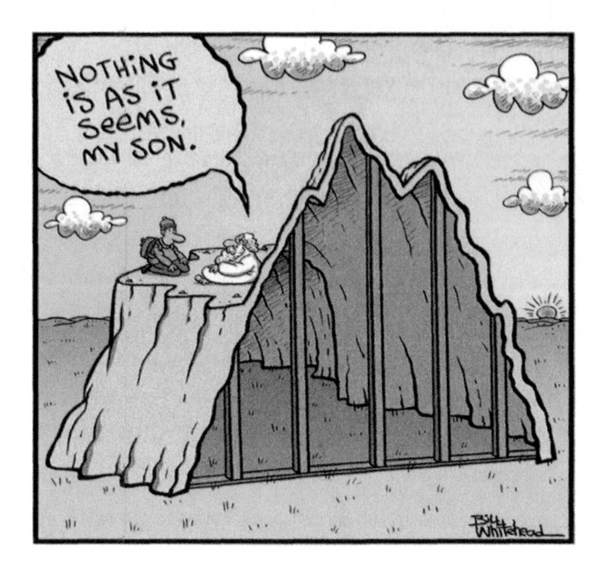

I am the first to acknowledge that this self-journey of finding and remembering your true Self can be a difficult journey. Mankind has been on this quest on an individual basis for all of history. From the proverbial mystic who sits on the mountain top contemplating and meditating on how to reach enlightenment; to Gautama Siddhartha, who lived a life of luxury and wealth, and set off on a journey of human suffering and pain until he became the Buddha; to Mahatma Gandhi who was deeply invested in his body and the drama of life, only to give it all up and seek the path of peace and enlightenment that positively affected millions of people for generations to come; to Mother Theresa who became a worldwide influencer of peace, enlightenment, and spiritual truth even though she eschewed all worldly pleasures and wealth for a life of working for the poorest and most wretched people on the planet by simply loving and caring for them. Yes, it can be a very, very difficult path to meet your true Self on your own personal journey to the truth. I do, however, maintain that because of your free will to choose the right-minded path to your enlightenment, your path does not necessarily have to be difficult and wrought with suffering, pain, and tragedy.

I think a wonderful example of this is the personal journey of one of the 20th and 21st century's most prolific self-help gurus, is Dr. Wayne Dyer. In the 1970's Dyer was a professor of psychology at St. John's University in New York. For a time, he was like any other professor working to gain tenure, but then he wrote his first book, *Your Erroneous Zones*, which became an international best seller. Along with his best-selling book came the accompanying fame including doing the mandatory rounds on all of the national radio and TV talk shows. Around this same time, a higher spiritual calling took hold of him, and despite his fair share of human drama in his lifetime – never knowing his father, divorce, leaving the university, and at one point later in his life, he was diagnosed with a form of leukemia, he continued to walk the path of enlightenment. By the time of his passing in 2015 at the age of 75, Wayne Dyer was probably considered to be one of the purest seekers and teachers of true spirituality and enlightenment in the world. Even at the time of his passing, many of his followers did not grieve, but simply rejoiced that Wayne had "graduated" to a higher level of enlightenment where he could continue his work. Along the way, his numerous self-help books on walking the spiritual path sparked a light in the hearts and minds of millions around the world. Here was a man, who lived a life filled with the usual human drama that would've sent anyone else into a spiral of depression, who was steadfast on his walk to find his real Self – the Self that stands as one with All-That-Is. Blessed with wealth, fame, and celebrity, Dyer never wavered as he used his free will to choose the right-minded path. In doing so, he became a true spiritual guru who was a beacon of light and hope to the people of the world. I think I can state with certainty that by the time Wayne Dyer had taken his last breath, he really had found his true Self.

The practical path to finding your true Self is exercising your free will and right to make the journey back home into the light. It's your choice to decide how and if you want to rediscover the power of your very real divine Self.

The Co-President of the Foundation for Inner Peace, the only authorized publisher of *A Course in Miracles*, Dr. Robert Rosenthal, authored the book, *From Never-Mind to Ever-Mind*, in which he notes what your journey to re-discovering your true self is like.

"A Course in Miracles states that all conflict and confusion in this world are ultimately the result of not knowing what we are – of forgetting, or intentionally diverting our minds and blocking it out. 'This is a course in how to know yourself.' The moment we remember our true Self (capitalized here because it is so much more than what we think of as self), *all our seeming problems are resolved, because they stem from this one source...the forgotten song of Self goes unheard. We remain ignorant of what we are, ever searching, never finding."*

3 Tools for Remembering Your True Self

Meditation is a great tool for your mind to clean out the debris of your thought systems to break into the clearing where the truth of your Self awaits.

There once was man who had suffered for many, many years with various psychological issues – anxiety, deep depression which led to thoughts of ending his own life, psychosis, and a deep lack of self-worth and self-confidence. After suffering the adversity of his negative mental conditions for a very long time, he reached the point where he knew that if he did not make some legitimate attempt to raise himself out of this mental downward spiral, he may not live much longer. Reaching down within himself he found a sparkle of light he had forgotten was in him and responded to an online ad he saw for a meditation class near where he lived. He was determined to take this positive step forward, and sure enough a couple days later he found himself at a local community events building sitting with five other meditation students and the class teacher. It was funny, he thought as he looked at the teacher's appearance as, for some reason he expected a full-blown Indian guru with a long-flowing beard and hair to be leading class. Instead this was a young woman, and she looked like any other lady he might see at the local shopping mall. With small, stifled laugh he let that image go as the class quickly fell into the quiet of the room that surrounded them, and he into his own thoughts – no earbuds, no music, no podcasts, no traffic sounds, no neighbors loudly shouting – just him and his thoughts. As he attempted to get his mind calm and quiet, he quickly heard within his head the loud, urgent, unsettling voice talking incessantly about this and that, and all of the thoughts that had led him down his dark mental pathway. Even though the only sound he heard was the deep breathing of the few other people that sat there meditating with him, he began to feel quite uneasy as the voice in his head, who he suddenly realized had been his lifelong companion, continued to chatter away nonstop. Suddenly, as if it was a gentle breeze had blown across his mind, and he heard the quiet voice of the class instructor say, "Now is the time to take a very deep breath, and as you exhale, release and let go the monkey mind of endless chatter that clutters your head. Keep taking those deep breaths and keep releasing that voice inside your head that won't shut up. You are in charge of your mind and your thoughts, not the monkey mind." And perhaps for the very first time in his life, suddenly this urgent, sometimes angry incessant voice, was no longer heard in his head. With that he found himself in a super quiet place of calm that he had never previously experienced – a calm that caused a small smile of contentment to crease his lips upward. As he settled into this sea of quiet and peace, suddenly he heard the monkey mind shout a single thought of, "Hey don't forget you have to go to the grocery store today and pick up those items for dinner!" Yet even as this happened, he suddenly realized that he had no interest in this random thought from his monkey mind. In his mind he simply watched this thought travel slowly across the screen of his mind, like when you sit at a railroad crossing and a train is going by in front of you. You patiently watch the train go by from one side of the screen of your vision to the other side, and then suddenly it's gone. Once he realized that he had the power to let this random thought simply go by and not let himself get sucked into it hook, line, and sinker, yet another smile, this time a little bigger, crossed his face. As the mediation session continued, more random monkey mind chatter and thoughts crossed his mind, but because he was less and less interested in their importance, they became fewer and farther between, until he was actually able to keep his mind almost totally quiet for many minutes at a time. At the peak of this very first experience of deep quiet and control of his own mind and thoughts, somewhere deep inside himself he thought he saw a flicker of light he never knew was there within him. At one point, but just for a moment or two, he thought he heard a choir way off in the distance singing a hymn, or at least he thought he did. Finally, the class came to an end as the teacher clasped her hands together, bowed, and softly said, "Namaste" to honor the students for showing up and sharing a mutual quiet time as a refuge from the chaos of the outside daily world. As the man left the building, he realized that for the first time in a very long time, and maybe for the first time ever, he had been free of the demanding, urgent voice that was always yelling in his head. He was swept into a lovely peace that he had forgotten was possible to exist in his mind.

Prayer is another practical tool to utilize on your journey to find your true self. Prayer is the next natural step, because meditation sets the stage by preparing that quiet, internal chatter-free mind that will help to make it effective.

"The part of your mind in which truth abides is in constant communication with God, whether you are aware of it or not. It is the other part of your mind that functions in the world and obeys the world's law's. It is this part that is constantly distracted, disorganized and highly uncertain. The part that is listening to the Voice for God is calm, always at rest and wholly certain. It is really the only part there is. The other part is a wild illusion, frantic and distraught, but without reality of any kind."

A Course in Miracles

Once again, especially for those of you who were raised in a religious household and identity, upon hearing the word "prayer", it's easy to think this is about religion, which is not necessarily true. Honestly, it really doesn't matter if you pray from a religious aspect or from a purely spiritual aspect. Prayer is all about communicating with the Supreme Being and joining with Him as one. Of course, many people consider prayer as a way to get God to give you the stuff you want – money, a new home, the perfect partner, to pass that algebra test, etc. Ideally, however, prayer is a way for you to simply join with God in pure communication. Yes, much of the time prayer does drift into asking God to help us attain our goals and dreams – that's ok. As opposed to just having God act like an amazon delivery truck dropping off your order right on your doorstep, prayer is really a wonderful avenue of communicating with God, but then releasing it by turning it all over to Him. Then you simply trust that that which you desire will be given you at the right time, in the right way, and in a way that will be the greatest benefit for all involved. At this point of letting go, prayer is similar to meditation in that your mind becomes quiet, because you are now in true commune with God. This is where miracles happen. I love how Gary Renard finishes a prayer by saying, "Now Father, I simply get lost in your love" and then sits quietly in trust and love.

Perhaps one of the best examples of utilizing prayer in a right-minded manner comes from St. Francis of Asissi.

The Prayer of Saint Francis of Assisi

Lord, make me an instrument of Thy peace;
Where there is hatred, let me sow love;
Where there is injury, pardon;
Where there is error, the truth;
Where there is doubt, the faith;
Where there is despair, hope;
Where there is darkness, light;
And where there is sadness, joy.

O Divine Master,
Grant that I may not so much seek
To be consoled, as to console;
To be understood, as to understand;
To be loved as to love.
For it is in giving that we receive;
It is in pardoning that we are pardoned;
And it is in dying that we are born to eternal life. Amen.

The Law of Attraction is yet another excellent tool for finding your true Self. However, as I have stated throughout this book, it can only be effective in a happy, healthy, and joyful manner if you have solidified your 3 Pillars and the foundation of your life. This can only come about via your consistent right-minded thinking based on those eternal universal principles I've taught you about. The principles of the L.O.A., of course, also walk hand-in-hand with both meditation and praying. With both, you are radiating energy (which is impossible for you to *not* do), and therefore continuously aligning with more of the same energy in the universe. The L.O.A. then orchestrates and sends more of it to you. If you seek to find your life's purpose and follow that path to finding your true Self, you would be wise to utilize the Law of Attraction in happy, loving way to stay on course and not fall by the wayside.

In the book, *Ask and It Is Given*, by Ester and Jerry Hicks, is a powerful statement of your ability to attract and create what you desire.

...you have the ability to always follow your true nature to pour through you, and that as you learn to consciously allow your full connection with the You that is your Source (your true Self), *your experience will be one of absolute joy. By consciously choosing the direction of your thoughts, you can be in constant connection with Source Energy* (the Law of Attraction/Universe)."

This is a beautiful statement that reveals the power of your true Self to attract, as it says above, "constant connection", or in becoming a consistent, deliberate creator of your own life. This is because you are consistently aligned with your Source Energy, All-That-Is – God.

The subtitle of this book, *A Beautiful Symbiotic Relationship*, of course, references to true spirituality and the Law of Attraction, and I believe that when you combine these three tools correctly as you seek your true Self, you will never fail to reach your goal. However, any of the three – meditation, prayer, and the Law of Attraction, will diminish in power and effectiveness when influenced and misused because you allowed the ego mind to slip back in and chatter away. Doing so will pull you off course, and your ship will end up on the rocks by the shore, the pillars of your being will collapse, and your personal foundation will crumble and return to the dust from whence it came. To prevent this, you must be diligent in directing your thoughts to stay on the path of right-mindedness that takes you directly to your true Self. Follow this path, and you will find that what the A.C.I.M. says to be true.

"The term 'right-mindedness' is properly used as the correction for 'wrong-mindedness,' and applies to the state of mind that induces accurate perception. It is miracle-minded because it heals misperception, and this is indeed a miracle in view of how you perceive yourself."

The tools are there for you – *meditation, prayer, and the Law of Attraction*, to utilize in in an appropriate, right-minded manner on your journey to Self, however, don't forget your power of choice. Each time you enter the realm of these three powerful tools, you must always exercise your free will, and choose between the false path of the ego constantly trying to pull you down to your eventual demise, or the path that leads to Heaven where the *real* you resides – your Self.

Chapter 16:

FOCUS, FAITH, TRUST – REPEAT!

"For every thousand people hacking at the leaves of evil, there is one striking at the roots."

Henry David Thoreau

I know many, many spiritual students who have spent thousands and thousands of dollars in attending self-help workshop after workshop. Their bookshelves overflow with hundreds of books on how to implement self-love, power affirmations, easy steps to your new life, find the key to happiness, and becoming an urban guru, yet they *still* don't get it. Even after attending all of these workshops and sitting at the feet of all of the self-help masters, somehow, they refuse (most of the time, unconsciously) to implement everything they've been taught, into their life.

"To know and not do, is to not know."
Chinese proverb

I will be the first to admit that for way too long I have been one of those people myself. You can apply all the classic lines to this perplexing tendency – spinning your wheels, taking one step forward and two steps back, this stuff doesn't work, I've wasted my time and money, why does this stuff work for others but not for me?

Fortunately, like many things in life, you finally just get fed up with making no progress toward what seems to be what you want, and you just finally go for it. At some point during your frustration of not being able to help yourself with all the self-help elements, you realize that somewhere deep inside, you value something that is incongruous with the picture of the happy, successful person you think you want to be. This deeper, hidden motive for your life usually sits in the ego-directed wrong-mindedness, where you have confused pain with pleasure, sacrifice with piousness, and anger with righteousness.

In keeping with the underlying main theme of this book, that is, creating a rock-solid personal foundation with strong-for-the-ages pillars, based on the positive, productive use of the Law of Attraction and the truth of unconditional love and oneness – I propose this simple, four-word instruction to make this your reality...

Focus, Faith, Trust – Repeat!

As we have seen, Quantum Physics and spiritual teachings, such as *A Course in Miracles*, have cited over and over that what you *focus* upon consistently and repeatedly will result in what becomes your reality. This concept is in perfect resonance and harmony with the Law of Attraction. When, where, how, and on what you focus on consistently with the very power of your thoughts, words and actions, can affect everything in your life – from the tiniest thing like what to eat for lunch to the biggest, most important aspect of your life, like your health. The constant *focus* of your attention will most definitely activate the attention of the Universe.

Anita Moorjani's revelation in her book, *Dying to Be* Me, on how and why she got cancer because of her constant fearful focus on the disease, is quite an eye-opener.

"The most frequent question people ask me is why I think I got cancer. I can sum it up in one word – fear. After my best friend, Soni, and Danny's brother-in-law were both diagnosed with cancer, I started to develop a deep fear of the disease. I felt that if it could strike them, it could strike anyone, so I began to do everything I could to keep from getting sick. However, the more I read about prevention, the more I felt I had reason to be afraid. Slowly, I found myself terrified of both dying and living. It was almost as if I was caged by my fears. My experience of life was getting smaller and smaller because, to me, the world was a menacing place. And then I was diagnosed with cancer."

Her testimony on the shear attracting power of her fearful focus resulted as cancer in her body really highlights what I have stated many times over – pay attention to what and how your thoughts are focusing on in every moment! If they stray into an area of that which you are fearful of, instantly use the power of your freedom of choice. Choose a better feeling, happy and healthier thought as quickly as possible. Let this new higher vibrating, better feeling thought be the focus of your attention. If you do not change the direction of your thoughts to that higher positive feeling energetic place then the eventual resulting manifestation can and will cause you to be the creator of your life by default, usually with negative results.

Focus can be defined as directed attention while *intent* is a clearly formulated act, thought or words (or combination of all three) that is directed at achieving a particular desired result. These are two very powerful words, especially when we are utilizing them to create and manifest all the good things that you would like to be, do or have. But, as we have seen, focus and intention can also be directed to the very opposite of the good things. This is classic Law of Attraction objectivity at work. Once you have gained clarity on the direction of your thoughts and you don't like their direction, then by choice – your inherent free will to choose – you can then turn the focus of your attention to the intention of creating the positive results you desire. This is yet another dynamic example of your power to create and mold your life the way you wish to. Once you start wielding this powerful combination of focus and intent, use it wisely for it will create the path on which your life traverses.

The second element, *faith* also wields great power, but sadly is vastly underestimated. This is because the most of mankind has been led to believe that faith is yet another one of those spiritual "woo" factors, and with the attached prevalent paradigm of "I'll believe it when I see it" mentality. The lack of belief in faith can be compared to why people do not believe something is real, simply because they can't see it within the spectrum of light in which their eyes are capable of seeing. The result of this attitude again is, "I don't see it, so I don't believe it"!

I'll use a personal story of faith as an example.

Even as a young man, I somehow sensed via what I call intuitive blind faith that I am always taken care of by my Source. This intuitive blind faith of mine has served me well and stayed with me for my entire life. I mentioned early in this book that in 1996 to 1997 I successfully ran 52 marathons in 52 weeks to raise money and awareness for leukemia, and I can most definitely report that I could never have accomplished it without faith. That year involved me driving 65,000 miles by myself, and 60,000 miles of flying to get to all 52 races. The places I ended up in, the situations I encountered, the heartbreaks, the extended, non-stop physical effort, the determination I needed, the successes, the disappointments, the massive support I received truly was beyond description – and I could never have accomplished it without my faith that I could and would somehow do it. When I headed off to marathon number one, the Cleveland Marathon on May 5, 1996, I simply did not have nearly enough money to do what I was setting out to do, *but* I had faith! I simply had pure, unadulterated, down to my bones, in my heart faith that the way would be made clear for me to accomplish it all for 52 weeks straight, plus in doing so make a positive difference in the world by helping to find a cure for leukemia. I really can't enumerate the number of times I rolled into yet another city in yet another state, or a new country (Canada), and had only a few dollars in my pocket and no idea where I would be staying the night – only to leave a couple days later with more than enough money to keep going, and a slew of new friends and supporters who felt like family to me who encouraged me to keep going. There is no other way I can explain it other than my complete faith that I was truly being taken care of and guided every single step of the way was how I was able to accomplish it. There was also the fact that, although I was in great physical shape, there was nothing extraordinary about my running ability except I had a lot of endurance, and my faith that I could and would accomplish my 52 in 52, never wavered. I had faith that I could, I would, and I did.

Obviously running 52 marathons in 52 weeks is an extreme example of one person's faith, but it really is a fantastic exhibit of the power of having faith. Even before I ever heard about *A Course in Miracles*, and read line one of the book, *"There is no order of difficulty in miracles"*, I learned of the truth of this statement because of my faith that I am always taken care of and guided safely and lovingly by my Source.

I'll add just one more personal story of faith in action that isn't quite so extreme, yet still very telling.

A while ago, I caught on that I was being given a particular message of guidance. It started in the morning when I received a regular e-mail from The Foundation for Inner Peace, (the organization that publishes the modern spiritual guide, *A Course in Miracles*) The e-mail basically told me, "Do not to look back. Keep my sight looking ahead, and don't dwell on the past."

So, I thought that was cool, and went on my way into my day. Later that morning, I was out on a dirt and gravel path in a public park doing my daily run, and a family passed me as they rode bikes. The final two bike riders that went by me were the little daughter (who was trying to turn around and look at her dad behind her, while she was riding, but she was weaving around as she attempted this). As her dad, who was riding right behind her, passed by me, he said out loud to her, "Don't look back. Keep looking ahead!"

Within a few seconds of hearing him say this, I suddenly realized that my Divine Guide was again speaking to me the same message I had read in the e-mail only a couple hours earlier. "Keep looking forward! Don't ever look back!"

If you make a conscious effort to tune your inner ear, eyes, and mind to the constant flow of Divine guidance that comes to each and every one of us, you really can get the message – the guidance that is meant to direct you down the path of your highest aspirations, dreams, desires, and safety.

I write this to give you hope, too. You too can escape the endless cycle of running from what you fear, and from the seemingly inescapable world of lack and attack. All you have to do is take that mighty leap of *faith*, and I guarantee you that your Divine Source will be/is there, waiting for you with open, loving arms.

I offer you this little affirmation that I wrote and posted on my refrigerator door that day, *"I move confidently forward in complete trust and faith, always looking forward, and never looking back."*

I know this is a deeply personal sharing on my part of what *faith* is and can be – and of course, your version of *faith* will be very personal to you too – but I am quite happy to share this experience of mine with you. I do so to give you an example of the true power of *faith* to create the life you desire.

The obvious ramifications in true spiritual terms of *faith* also stands out. *Faith* opens up and blossoms with the beauty of a white lily, as you put your focus and intention on a very real power that you can't see with your body's eyes. Once you establish your faith in your Source, in All-That-Is, that adds yet another solid layer to the personal foundation of your life. It is something you can count on to be there when you need it, with results that will always be for your highest good and well-being.

The third element for helping you to create strong and powerful personal foundation for your life is *trust*.

"There is one thing that is common to every individual…If developed and leveraged, that one thing has the potential to create unparalleled success and prosperity in every dimension of life. Yet, it is the least understood, most neglected, and most underestimated possibility of our time. That one thing is trust."

Stephen M.R. Covey, from The Speed of Trust

Let's face it, we don't live in a very trusting world. The word *trust* can be and has been misused in every way possible. How many times have we heard someone lacking integrity say, "Trust me on this" which of course, instantly causes us to not trust them. And then there's the disappointment factor. I'm sure there are many times in your life (especially when you were young) you put your trust in someone or something, and the result you desired didn't happen. When this happens, your faith in the use of trust, especially in important moments and situations in your life, is drastically reduced. This is the cause of cynicism in many people, which then results in a lower, negative, and dis-empowering level of your personal energy, which then begat the "I'll believe it when I see it" syndrome. As a matter of fact, just look around you in the world, especially when you watch TV, there's not a whole lot of trust happening in this world. There is a serious shortage of trust on planet earth, when the truth is there's an unlimited supply of trust available that would fill every single person's "trust cup" to overflowing. It's like your true Self, we have simply forgotten that it is there – always, just simply waiting for you to take a hold of it and T-R-U-S-T.

So, let me again relay another personal encounter of mine, this one in how I came to embrace and implement this important element called *trust*. I call this story, "The Trust Monkey".

The longer I live, and as I continue my journey of spiritual enlightenment and awakening, the more I realize that I just never know when, where or how inspiration will come from.

I've been inspired and motivated by downtrodden people who have risen way above what was thought possible of them. I have been inspired by a momentary glimpse of the stunning beauty of a flower blossoming in a ray of morning sunshine as I rushed by it during my daily run. I've been inspired, charmed, and enlightened by a baby duckling.

And now my latest inspiration comes from my own silly sense of humor!

OK, I admit it, I've always had a different perspective on things, and my sense of humor can seem downright childish much of the time, but, darn it, I take my inspiration where I can get – and Lord knows, we need all the inspiration we can get in a world that seems to be based on lack, guilt, fear, and attack!

So, I give you (drum roll please!) The Trust Monkey! Ha ha! Like I said, a fairly childish, simplistic effort on my part, but it works for me, that is. Here's how the Trust Monkey came into being a couple of days ago.

I was at the end of a long, tiring day, and before I was about to turn in for the night, I came across a trinket left over from a holiday dinner party I was at this past year at a friend's house. It was a little, painted glass monkey with a metal place card holder sticking out of its head, meant for the hostess to easily put a name card in so you knew where to sit at the table.

As I left the dinner party at night's end, she gave me a stash of awesome food, cookies, etc. to take home with me. When I got home and opened this bag of goodies, I found the little glass monkey, and I placed it in my kitchen cupboard and forgot about it...that is until this night when it returned to my sight.

For many days I had been reading quite a bit about trust. I've also written a fair amount about trust. Trust is something that I have been trying to develop and integrate in myself. Trust in my Source, in the Universe, in All That Is, in the eternally flowing Stream of Wellbeing.

I've come to understand that "trust" actually means "consistency" in believing and knowing that I am always taken care of and lovingly watched over by The Creator, and when I trust in this knowing, it increases in power, and moves to a higher vibrating place of Love.

As a Law of Attraction Life Coach, I've come to know and live by the beauty and simplicity of understanding that "like attracts like". I have also come to experience that as I consistently trust in the Universal Truths of Love and Light, so too does the feeling of pure peace that I am truly taken care of at every moment.

This is a very freeing feeling! So, with sleepy eyes, and mind, I pulled out my marker, and simply printed the word "TRUST" on a small piece of paper, and stuffed it into the monkey's name cardholder, put it on my desk in my bedroom, and hit the sack for the night.

The next morning, I woke up feeling unusually refreshed, and as I walked over to my desk and turned the light on, the first thing I saw was The Trust Monkey! I just started laughing and laughing, and grinning from ear-to-ear, and that is how I started my day.

As I drank my morning cup of java, I kept thinking about and occasionally walking over to look at this silly little Trust Monkey and kept laughing! How simplistic! How seemingly silly, but it's not silly. It's absolutely wonderful that I can find something like this to immediately and lovingly remind me that I always trust in my Source!

And when I look at it, I laugh not because it's dumb (at least not to me), but because I know that I am completely and lovingly taken care of by All-That-Is. Not only that, it also puts me in a good mood and makes me smile, ready to roll into my day to hopefully inspire others to trust, too.

So wherever and however you do it, find or make your own form of a "Trust Monkey" as a constant reminder to yourself that your true, Divine Self is always, always taken care of and loved, bathed in the Light of your Source, and always flowing downstream in the Stream of Wellbeing! The Trust Monkey has spoken – T-R-U-S-T!

Yes, the Trust Monkey has spoken! The one thing he would have you understand is that these three key elements of your life – focus, faith, and trust are interlocked. *Focus* on what you desire brings *faith* that it will happen, and all of it is supported by your *trust* in the whole process. The one very important thing you must remember about your usage of these three elements is that the results you seek may not, and usually don't occur exactly as you may have pictured it in your heart and mind. This is where you cannot allow yourself to slip into disappointment. When you get the results, but not exactly as you had imagined it, be grateful! When this happens, it is one of the beauties of how the Universe functions. You will *always* receive want you want in a form that is designed for your overall greatest good and all involved. How many times have we all heard someone express disappointment and even anger at something that didn't turn out the way they thought it should have, only to hear them say (sometimes years later) that the result that initially looked like a disaster, was really the best thing that could have ever happened to them!

A great example of this is a friend of mine from my youth who one day was called into the manager's office at his place of employment. He went in with every expectation of hearing his boss tell him he had been promoted. Instead, he left the office in near tears as he found out that he had just been fired! For a long time after this seeming "disaster", my friend was bitter and cynical about the whole incident, but as time went on it became obvious to those of us who were his friends that his getting fired was the best thing that could have happened to him at that time! It was the exact kick-in-the-butt he needed that spurred him on to go live a life doing what he *really* loved as his life and career. Had he received that promotion instead of getting fired, he might have remained mired in a mediocre job doing something he only enjoyed a little bit. This is an excellent example of the Universe delivering your desires in a manner and form that is best for your well-being and for everyone involved that is not immediately and readily apparent.

Stories like these should really make you aware of just how and why your focus, faith, and trust are *so* important.

"Sometimes life serves as our shaman and sets up situations that completely destroy our old dream. Death, divorce, the loss of a job are all things that require us to go out into the wilderness, taking with us very few of our possessions, and find a new dream. But our home, our truth, is always inside us, and we take that with us wherever we go."

Don Jose Miguel, The Wisdom of the Shaman

And finally, there's the necessary action you must take to solidify the elements of focus, faith, and trust – *repetition.*

Once you start repeating your statements of your belief in focus, faith, and trust over, and over, and over, and then repeat them some more, this is where you start changing the vibrational frequency of the energy of your being – the energy frequency that you are sending out to the universe. This repetition is so very key in your ultimate success in creating what you desire in your life, because it can take some time for you to change your lower, unproductive energetic frequency that you've been vibrating at for a very long time – sometimes for an entire lifetime!

Let me use the example of an old-fashioned radio. Before digital technology made push-buttons possible, most older radios had a big knob on the front. To change from one station to another, you had to turn this knob so that the station indicator moved across the dial until you found the one you wanted to hear. If you had been listening to a station at 88.9 MHz but wanted to then listen to the station at 107.9 MHz (on the opposite side of the dial), you had to slowly and surely turn the tuning knob all the way from one side of the dial to the other side until you found the station you wanted to listen to. In other words, it took some time and effort to change the frequency to the one you wanted it to be. And even once you found the frequency of the station you wanted to listen to, you still then had to fine-tune the station indicator on the radio until you got it exactly where it received the signal at its loudest, clearest, and most powerful point! This is exactly what you need to do with that which you desire to create and manifest into your life – tune in to its vibrational energy frequency, and then keep fine-tuning it until it is in perfect alignment with the vibrational energy frequency of your desire, of your being.

If you have been in a low vibrating, negative, and unproductive energetic mindset for the last 35 years, believe me, it is going to take that time and effort on your part in slowly and surely repeating over and over and over and over your statements of your focus, faith, and trust. Then you will eventually start to notice a higher vibrating, more positive, productive change in the energetic frequency of your being as the things you really desired to be in your life start to show up – *this* is where miracles happen! There is a vortex of energy that hovers over your being where all the energy of your thoughts, words, and actions, and the energy of your heart reside along with all of your true, unconscious desires (the part that the universe hears and feels the strongest emanating from you). Brendan D. Murphy's, *The Grand Illusion, Book One*, states,

"Gregg Braden (along with a myriad of others) also emphasizes the crucial role played by the heart in manifesting and co-creating our experiences at this level of reality. He emphasizes that in making our intention known, we must 'drop' into the field of the heart and actually feel gratitude – it is this emotion that is so powerful in drawing to us what we desire."

As you continue your repetitions of focus, faith, and trust, your vortex energy (known by scientists and researchers as a *torsional field*) starts its metamorphosis to a higher vibrating, more loving, happy, healthy, and abundant place of existence.

Again, referring to Murphy's book, "*Various researchers consider torsion as being synonymous or identical with consciousness itself. Since torsion waves are a fundamental and ubiquitous feature of the cosmos, we can see how consciousness is also; consciousness has a real and detectable 'energy' that is distinguishable from gravity and electromagnetism.*"

This may be exactly why some individuals such as empaths, who are highly sensitive to the energy of other people, testify that they can see an aura of light and feel the power of their radiating field of energy (vortex or torsional field).

Think of how the media and businesses utilize the power of repetition via their advertising and in messages they want to drive home to you. Therefore, you may see a TV commercial for a new laundry detergent over a hundred times in a month, and the message of the ad slowly but surely seeps into your subconscious. Next time you head to your local grocery store and head down the detergent aisle, you suddenly reach for a bottle of this new detergent almost without thinking. So, if the repetition of a TV commercial is so powerful in subconsciously changing your buying habits, think of just how powerful the repetition of the affirmations of your focus, faith, and trust can be!

"Whatever we plant in our subconscious mind and nourish with repetition and emotion will one day become a reality."

- Earl Nightingale

If you take a hold of and practice these essential elements of focus, faith, trust, and continue to multiply their power via continuous repetition, I will guarantee that you will get the results that you wish to have manifest into your life. But as I have pointed out throughout this entire book, you will vastly improve the chances of success in the achievement of your desires and goals if you stand upon the podium of integrity of right-minded thinking, speaking, and actions. Yes, there probably is a decent chance that you may achieve success in your manifestations even if your pillars and foundation have a couple big cracks in them, but you will not reach the goal of having your "house", your life, stand strong for the ages because of it. Remember, any "cracks" in your life will almost *always* lead to your entire life or some key areas of your life, to come crashing down into the dust. Unfortunately, it is when your life comes crashing down around you that what you thought was worth taking the risk of doing at the time, suddenly becomes apparent that it was not worth it after all – but then it's too late.

Chapter 17:

PUTTING IT ALL TOGETHER

"Ne te quaesiveris extra"

"Man is his own star; and the soul than can
Render an honest and perfect man,
Commands all light, all influence, all fate;
Nothing to him falls early or too late.
Our acts our angels are, or good or ill,
Out fatal shadows that walk by us still."

Epilogue to Beaumont and Fletcher's Honest Man's Fortune (taken from Ralph Waldo Emerson's essay on Self-Reliance)

The Latin phrase, "Ne te quaesiveris extra" – "Do not look outside yourself" is truly an excellent way to start this chapter on putting it all together – putting your 3 Pillars, and your Keystone of Forgiveness upright and strong, all standing on the rock-solid foundation of your life.

This entire book, to this point, is all about ne te quaesiveris extra – do not look outside of yourself to build a strong, healthy, joyful, happy, and abundant life.

By now you should understand that (as *A Course in Miracles* calls them) the Great Rays still reside within you shining and radiating out to the universe with the blinding brilliance of a super nova! This is the very life force you were born with, instilled in you by God who created you as His Holy Son that you are. The darkness of the world and the ego may obscure them with a thick curtain of forgetfulness and uncertainty, but the Great Rays can *never* be diminished even an iota, because they are your Self.

By now you should understand that it is possible for you to be a victim of circumstances or other people, only if you allow it to occur.

By now you should be completely certain that you, (and I stated this at the very beginning of this book but needs further emphasizing) only *you* are the writer, producer, and director of your life – *no one else,* only *you!*

Not only are you the carpenter, mason, and construction worker who built your personal foundation and 3 Pillars strong-for-the-ages, but you are also the sole screenwriter of how your life plays out. Will it unfold in a beautiful, successful, healthy, and happy manner, or will it unravel in mental illness, physical and mental abuse, and even suicide?

By now you have remembered that you *always* have the power and free will to choose the right-minded integrity of walking with and living in harmony with the eternal universal truths of love and oneness. In doing so your life will be a journey filled with the brilliant light of your Creator who knows no darkness and shares all that He has with you, His Son.

When you walk in the integrity of these universal truths, you simply cannot go astray. If you do, then you know that you took a wrong step, or a wrong turn somewhere along the path of your life. And even if you do make a misstep, there is beauty in knowing that The Father will *never* abandon you, but instead will pick you up from your fall, brush the dirt and dust from your clothes, and then lovingly whisper in your ear, *"My Son, choose again."*

At this point you now understand that utilizing true, non-dualistic teachings and principles of these universal truths in unison with your knowledge of how simply, easily, and omnisciently the Law of Attraction orchestrates the way for you to live the life you really want to live.

Now when you hear the harsh voice of the ego deriding you, calling you names, trying to make you believe you are a failure and are not, nor will you ever be, worthy of having your greatest dream, your best life, you will stand strong. Because the Light still burns brightly within your Self, and the Great Rays shine out into eternity, you can simply laugh as the ego attempts to derail you, and gently blow it away with a whoosh of air to dissipate the veil of smoke it used to obscure your Light and the Truth.

When you do reach that last moment and your last breath within this body you were given during this lifetime, you will have no regrets, no wish for a "do-over", because you built your life on an immovable personal foundation supported by your mental, physical, and spiritual pillars that are forever strong. And when you exhale your very last breath, instead of your "house", your life crashing into the ground in the ceremony of "ashes to ashes, dust to dust", your life simply assumes its true Self as the Great Rays that waited for this moment, return you to your home with your Father.

"According to A Course in Miracles and mystics of all traditions, the goal of the spiritual journey is enlightenment, salvation, awakening from the ego's nightmare to perfection of light, love, peace, timelessness, holiness, and presence. This experience is far closer to reality – the real world that the Course describes – than the fleeting interval between birth and death that we label life."

Dr. Robert Rosenthal, From Never-Mind to Ever-Mind

Printed in Great Britain
by Amazon